Primal Paleo Cookbook

Quick and Easy Paleo Recipes

Primal Paleo Cookbook

Quick and Easy Paleo Recipes

DYLANNA**PRESS**

Copyright © 2014 by Dylanna Publishing, Inc.
All rights reserved. This book or any portion thereof may not be reproduced or used in any manner whatsoever without the express written permission of the publisher except for the use of brief quotations in a book review.

First edition: 2014

Disclaimer/Limit of Liability

This book is for informational purposes only. The views expressed are those of the author alone, and should not be taken as expert, legal, or medical advice. The reader is responsible for his or her own actions.

Every attempt has been made to verify the accuracy of the information in this publication. However, neither the author nor the publisher assumes any responsibility for errors, omissions, or contrary interpretation of the material contained herein.

This book is not intended to provide medical advice. Please see your health care professional before embarking on any new diet or exercise program. The reader should regularly consult a physician in matters relating to his/her health and particularly with respect to any symptoms that may require diagnosis or medical attention.

Contents

Introduction 1
    About the Paleo Diet 1
    Health Benefits of the Paleo Diet 2
Stocking Your Paleo Kitchen 5
7-Day Paleo Meal Plan 9

Part II - Recipes 13

Breakfast and Egg Dishes 15
Poultry Dishes 35
Meat Dishes (Beef, Pork, and Lamb) 55
Seafood Dishes 85
Vegetables, Fruits, and Salads 113
Soups and Stews 133
Sauces, Dips, and Condiments 145
Desserts, Treats, and Snacks 155
From the Author 171

Index 175

Introduction

WHETHER you're just starting out on the Paleo diet or have been eating Paleo for years, the *Primal Paleo Cookbook: Quick and Easy Paleo Recipes* is going to help you make delicious, healthy meals without spending a lot of time in the kitchen.

This book was designed for people who want to be able to get their meals on the table fast, without the need for a lot of special ingredients or difficult cooking techniques. These recipes feature fresh, whole foods that are cooked the Paleo way—without refined sugars, processed foods, or unhealthy oils. They're perfect for those days you come home tired from work and need to get dinner on the table without a lot of fuss, using ingredients you already have on hand. Or when you want to put everything into a slow cooker and then set it and forget it.

In addition to more than 100 Paleo recipes, also included in the book is a brief overview of the Paleo diet—what it is, the health benefits of eating the Paleo way, how to stock your Paleo kitchen, and a 7-day Paleo meal plan. For a more in-depth look at the Paleo diet and how to get started with it, see the *Paleo Diet: Beginner's Paleo Cooking for Health and Weight Loss*.

About the Paleo Diet

The Paleo, or Paleolithic, diet is a way of eating that attempts to mimic as much as possible the diet and eating habits of humans during the pre-agricultural, or Paleolithic era. It is also known as the Stone Age diet, the hunter-gatherer diet, and the caveman diet. The focus of the diet is eating foods as close to their natural states as possible. The mainstays are organic, grass-fed meat, poultry, wild game, seafood, and fresh vegetables and fruits.

The theory behind the diet is simple. It reasons that humans evolved over the course of 2.5 million years during a time when there was no agriculture and thus no grains, dairy products, legumes, processed foods, or refined sugars. Therefore, the human digestive system and nutritional needs are best adapted to the diet and foods that were eaten by our ancestors for hundreds of thousands of years. Modern humans have not yet adapted fully to the types of foods that have become available since the agricultural revolution which took place approximately

10,000 years ago. This maladaptation has led to many of the health problems we see today including diabetes, heart disease, obesity, and autoimmune disorders such as celiac disease and IBS.

Eating the Paleo way is not so much a diet as a lifestyle choice. If you want the long-term health benefits that the Paleo diet provides, then you need to be prepared to commit to it long-term. Yes, the occasional non-Paleo treat is okay, but for the most part, this is a style of eating that requires commitment.

Health Benefits of the Paleo Diet

There are many benefits to following the Paleolithic way of eating. Once you cut out processed foods, grains, and refined sugars, most people find they have never felt healthier. In addition to increased energy levels, the Paleo diet can help with weight loss, improve cholesterol levels, reduce triglycerides in the blood, stabilize blood sugar, and reduce inflammation throughout the body.

Why so many health benefits from the Paleo diet? Perhaps it is because the focus is on eating real food, without a lot of additives. By cutting out grains, dairy, sugar, and processed foods and adding in more fruits and vegetables, you will be dramatically increasing your intake of vitamins, minerals, and antioxidants.

Another reason the Paleo diet is good for your health is its focus on healthy fats. Specifically omega-3 fatty acids, or polyunsaturated fatty acids (PUFAs). In a typical American diet the ratio of omega-6 fatty acids to omega-3 fatty acids can be as high as 15 to 1. This is in stark contrast to the recommended 1 to 1 ratio. This imbalance is due to our reliance on processed foods that are filled with refined vegetable oils, such as soybean oil, which are composed of omega-6 fatty acids. This imbalance can lead to chronic, systemic inflammation and is implicated in a host of diseases included asthma, cancer, heart disease, autoimmune disease, and obesity. By following the Paleo diet, you will balance this ratio and reverse the detrimental effects of the disproportionate level of omega-6s.

Another area where you will feel the benefits of the Paleo diet is in your gut health. By cutting out sugar, processed foods, and unhealthy fats, you will eliminate the main sources of stress and inflammation within your digestive tract. The natural bacteria that live in your intestinal system will thrive and you will have better overall gut health. Symptoms such as gas, bloating, constipation, diarrhea, and cramping will all be greatly relieved by following the Paleo way of eating.

Overall, when compared to the standard American diet (SAD), the Paleo diet is richer in nutrients and provides more of the micro- and macronutrients that the human body needs for optimum health. After following the Paleo diet, the majority of people report increased energy levels, better sleep quality, more stabilized moods, weight loss, better gut health, and a reduction in symptoms associated with inflammation including chronic pain, nasal congestion, and other allergic symptoms.

Stocking Your Paleo Kitchen

A BIG PART of preparing meals without a lot of fuss is having the ingredients you need on hand. Keeping your pantry stocked with a few essentials will go a long way toward making it easy to prepare a quick and healthy Paleo meal.

Cleaning Out

If you're committed to eating the Paleo way, the first thing you need to do is clean out your refrigerator, freezer, and pantry. Look carefully at all of the labels of everything in your kitchen. Get rid of anything that contains dairy, gluten, grains, legumes, sugar, and soy. Soy can be especially tricky to identify and is found in many types of products including the majority of processed foods.

Restocking

Now that you've gotten rid of all the foods that may be causing problems, it's time to stock up on a few basics to keep on hand.

Pantry Items

- Almond butter
- Almond flour
- Apple cider vinegar
- Apple sauce – no sugar added
- Arrowroot flour
- Avocado oil
- Baking soda
- Balsamic vinegar

- Broths – beef, chicken, vegetable, for times when you don't want to make homemade, buy organic, low-sodium
- Cacao powder/cacao nibs
- Coconut aminos – this is essential for making Asian-style and teriyaki dishes to use in place of soy sauce
- Coconut flour
- Coconut milk
- Coconut oil
- Dried fruits – apricots, cranberries, dates, goji berries, plums, raisins
- Dried mushrooms
- Fish sauce
- Ghee – make your own or purchase
- Herbs and spices– dried, grow your own fresh (allspice, black peppercorns, cardamom, cayenne pepper, cumin, ginger, oregano, thyme, garam masala, ground ancho chile, cinnamon, clove, red pepper flakes, paprika, curry powder, nutmeg, za'atar)
- Honey
- Lard
- Maple syrup
- Molasses
- Nut butters – almond, cashew, hazelnut, coconut
- Nut oils – almond, macadamia, walnut
- Nutritional yeast
- Nuts – raw cashews, almonds, macadamia, hazelnuts, pecans, pistachio, walnuts
- Olive oil
- Olives – green, black, Kalamata
- Pumpkin puree, canned (not pie filling)
- Rice vinegar
- Salmon, wild caught, canned
- Salsa
- Sardines
- Sea salt, Himalayan salt
- Tahini
- Tapioca starch
- Tomatoes – canned, paste, sauce
- Tuna, canned
- Vanilla extract
- White wine vinegar

Freezer items
- Bananas
- Berries
- Homemade soups and broth – freeze in single servings
- Meats
- Scallops
- Shrimp

Refrigerator items

- Bacon
- Eggs
- Fresh fruits and vegetables
- Garlic
- Lemons
- Limes
- Onions
- Salad greens

7-Day Paleo Meal Plan

PLANNING AHEAD is key to keeping things quick and easy. Spending a few minutes at the beginning of the week to map out your meals for the week ahead and making sure you have all the necessary ingredients ahead of time will save you lots of time during the week. Here is a 7-day Paleo meal plan to get you started.

Day One

- **Breakfast:** *Paleo Vegetable Omelet*
- **Lunch:** *Spiced Ginger Carrot Soup; Green Salad*
- **Afternoon Snack:** *Guacamole and veggie crudités*
- **Dinner:** *Pecan-Crusted Fish with Orange Sauce*
- **Dessert:** *Coconut Chocolate Truffles*

Day Two

- **Breakfast:** *Zucchini, Red Pepper, and Sweet Potato Frittata*
- **Lunch:** *Healthy, Yummy Real Tuna Salad*
- **Afternoon Snack:** *Kale Chips*
- **Dinner:** *Paleo Chili*
- **Dessert:** *Paleo Honey Cake*

Day Three

- **Breakfast:** *Egg white omelet with asparagus*
- **Lunch:** *Cran-Apple Chicken Salad*
- **Afternoon Snack:** *Hot Baked Cinnamon Apples*
- **Dinner:** *Slow-Cooked Pork Carnitas*
- **Dessert:** *Carrot Chocolate Cookies*

Day Four

- **Breakfast:** *Paleo Pumpkin Pancakes*
- **Lunch:** *Kale and Orange Salad with Cranberry Vinaigrette*
- **Afternoon Snack:** *Whole-Grain Walnut Cookies*
- **Dinner:** *Pan-Seared Salmon on Baby Arugula*
- **Dessert:** *Lemon Almond Meal Cake with Blueberry Cream*

Day Five

- **Breakfast:** *Easy Paleo Breakfast Scramble*
- **Lunch:** *Portobello Burger*
- **Afternoon Snack:** *1/2 cup of fresh berries; handful of nuts*

- **Dinner:** *Teriyaki Chicken Stir-Fry with Cauliflower Rice*

- **Dessert:** *Fudgy Chocolate Brownies*

Day Six

- **Breakfast:** *Banana Apple Smoothie with Greens*

- **Lunch:** *Egg Salad Lettuce Wraps*

- **Afternoon Snack:** *Paleo Pumpkin Muffin*

- **Dinner:** *Beef and Veggie Kebabs with Spicy Mediterranean Marinade*

- **Dessert:** *Honey Macaroons*

Day Seven

- **Breakfast:** *Baked Eggs with Tomatoes and Bacon*

- **Lunch:** *Shrimp and Avocado Ceviche*

- **Afternoon Snack:** *Curried Zucchini Chips*

- **Dinner:** *Glazed Pork Chops with Apricot-Mango Salsa*

- **Dessert:** *Coconut Date Bites*

Part Two

Recipes

Breakfast and Egg Dishes

Eating a healthy Paleo breakfast will provide you with enough energy to get you through your busy day. Eggs can also make a quick, nutritious, and versatile dinner.

Paleo Vegetable Omelet

An omelet makes a perfect breakfast, lunch, or even dinner on the Paleo diet. You can use whatever vegetables you have on hand and in just a few minutes be eating a healthy, high-protein meal.

Servings: 1

Ingredients

- 2-3 large eggs
- 1 tablespoon water
- 2 teaspoon olive oil
- 1/4 yellow onion, chopped
- 1/2 tomato, diced
- 2-3 asparagus stalks, cut into small pieces
- 3-4 mushrooms, sliced

Directions

1. Crack eggs into a bowl, add tablespoon of water, and whisk with fork until well blended.

2. Heat 1 teaspoon oil over medium-high heat in a medium size skillet. Add onion, tomato, asparagus, and mushrooms and sauté until vegetables are tender, about 3-4 minutes. Remove from pan and set aside.

3. Add another teaspoon of oil to the pan and allow to heat for a minute or two. Add beaten eggs to pan, tilting pan as needed so eggs cover entire pan. Let eggs set along edges of pan, this should only take a few seconds if pan is hot enough. Using spatula slide eggs away from sides of pan and tilt pan to allow more egg mixture to flow to pan surface. Repeat until eggs are almost finished, but still soft in the middle.

4. Add vegetable mixture to middle of omelet. Fold one side of omelet over toppings. Slide onto plate. Voila, it is ready to eat.

Zucchini, Red Pepper, and Sweet Potato Frittata

If you haven't tried making a frittata before, then you're going to love how easy it is to whip up a complete breakfast or light dinner. Similar to an omelet, but without the flip. You can use just about anything in your frittata, but this combination is colorful and delicious.

Servings: 4

Ingredients
- 2 teaspoons ghee or coconut oil
- 8 large eggs
- 1 medium sweet potato, peeled and sliced
- 1 large zucchini, sliced into thin rounds
- 1 red pepper, sliced thin
- 1 tablespoon fresh parsley, chopped
- Salt and pepper to taste

Directions

1. Heat ghee or coconut oil in pan over medium-high heat. Add sweet potato and cook until tender, 7-8 minutes.

2. Add zucchini and red pepper and continue cooking for another 4-5 minutes.

3. Crack eggs into bowl and whisk until eggs are well blended and frothy.

4. Pour eggs into pan with vegetable mixture. Season with salt and pepper.

5. Turn heat down to low and cook until eggs are just set, 8-10 minutes. Eggs will still be loose on top.

6. Remove pan from heat and place under hot broiler until frittata is golden brown on top.

7. Sprinkle with fresh parsley for garnish and serve.

Easy Paleo Breakfast Scramble

This super easy breakfast scramble is packed with protein and will keep you fueled all morning long.

Servings: 1

Ingredients

- 1 teaspoon ghee of coconut oil
- 2-3 large eggs
- 1 tablespoon water or coconut milk
- 2-3 slices Canadian bacon, cut into small pieces
- 1/2 small yellow onion, diced
- 1 small handful baby spinach, chopped
- Salsa for topping (optional)

Directions

1. Heat oil in medium-size pan over medium heat. Add Canadian bacon and onion and sauté for 3-4 minutes until onions start to soften. Add spinach and continue cooking until spinach is soft and wilted.
2. While bacon and veggies are cooking, crack eggs into bowl and add either 1 tablespoon water or coconut milk. Whisk eggs until well blended.
3. Turn heat down to low. Pour eggs over bacon and veggies. Cook, stirring frequently, until eggs are just set.
4. Remove eggs from heat onto plate. Top with salsa if desired. Eat at once.

Baked Eggs with Tomato and Bacon

Simple, easy, made all in one pan, what more can I say?

Servings: 2

Ingredients

- 6 slices bacon
- 4 eggs
- 1 cup cherry or grape tomatoes, halved
- 1 teaspoon dried oregano
- Salt and pepper, to taste

Directions

1. Preheat oven to 425 degrees.
2. Place bacon on baking sheet and cook for 12-15 minutes.
3. Remove pan from oven. Make room for eggs on pan. Crack eggs onto pan. Spread tomatoes around pan. Season with oregano, salt, and pepper.
4. Put pan back in oven and cook until bacon is crispy and eggs are cooked through, about 5-8 minutes.
5. Serve at once.

Coconut Flour Pancakes

When you get tired of eggs for breakfast give these grain-free, protein-packed pancakes a try.

Servings: 4

Ingredients

- 5 large eggs
- 1 cup applesauce, unsweetened
- 1/2 cup coconut flour
- 1 teaspoon baking soda
- 1 teaspoon vanilla
- 1 teaspoon cinnamon
- ghee or coconut oil for frying

Directions

1. Crack eggs into a bowl, add in applesauce, coconut flour, baking soda, vanilla, and cinnamon. Whisk until well blended.

2. Heat large skillet over medium-high heat. Add ghee or coconut oil to coat pan. When pan is hot, add 1/4 cup batter to pan for each pancake.

3. Cook until batter starts to bubble, about 2-3 minutes. Flip and cook until other side is light brown.

4. Serve topped with your favorite fruit, honey or real maple syrup.

Bacon and Egg Omelet Muffins

This recipe is super easy and always a hit for breakfast.

Servings: 12

Ingredients

- 1 pound bacon
- 1 yellow onion, diced
- 1 cup baby spinach, coarsely chopped
- 9 large eggs
- 1 teaspoon dried oregano
- Sea salt and freshly ground black pepper, to taste
- ½ cup coconut milk

Directions

1. Grease muffin tin. Preheat oven to 350 degrees.

2. Heat skillet over medium-high heat and add bacon. Cook until bacon is just cooked but not crisp. Remove from pan and drain on paper towels.

3. Add onion to skillet and sauté for 3-4 minutes or until onion are translucent. Add spinach to pan and sauté for another minute or so until spinach wilts.

4. Crack eggs into a large bowl and whisk until just mixed. Crumble in bacon. Add onion and spinach mixture, oregano, salt, pepper, and coconut milk. Stir until combined.

5. Spoon the egg mixture evenly into the muffin tins.

6. Bake in oven until eggs are firm, about 15-20 minutes.

Paleo Pumpkin Pancakes

Another version of pancakes that taste like the real thing. Delicious!

Servings: 4

Ingredients

- 1 cup almond flour
- 4 tablespoons coconut flour
- 2 tablespoons ground flax seed
- 1 teaspoon salt
- 1 tablespoon cinnamon
- 1/2 teaspoon baking soda
- 1 cup pumpkin puree
- 4 large eggs
- 4 tablespoons honey
- 1 teaspoon vanilla extract
- Ghee or coconut oil for frying

Directions

1. In a bowl, mix together almond flour, coconut flour, flax seed, salt, cinnamon, and baking soda.

2. In separate bowl, whisk together pumpkin, eggs, honey, and vanilla. Pour mixture into bowl with dry ingredients. Mix until well blended.

3. Heat large skillet over medium-high heat. Add ghee or coconut oil to coat pan. Pour 1/4 cup of batter per pancake onto pan.

4. Cook until batter starts to bubble, about 2-3 minutes. Flip over and cook until other side is light brown, about 1-2 minutes.

5. Serve topped with pure maple syrup.

Egg Salad

This a quick and easy egg salad recipe that makes a nice lunch or quick filling snack. Also works as a filling for stuffed tomatoes.

Servings: 2

Ingredients

- 4 large eggs, hard boiled
- 1 tablespoon Paleo mayonnaise
- 1 teaspoon spicy brown mustard
- 1/4 small red onion, minced
- Salt and pepper to taste
- Romaine lettuce leaves, for serving

Directions

1. Cut eggs into small pieces into a bowl.
2. Add mayonnaise, mustard, onion, salt, and pepper. Mix to combine.
3. Serve in lettuce leaf boats.

Coconut Fruit and Nut Granola

Make up a big batch of this granola and store in an airtight container. Makes a healthy, crunchy, and quick breakfast.

Servings: 8-10

Ingredients

- 3 cups unsweetened coconut flakes
- 2 cups almonds, roughly chopped
- 1 cup sunflower seeds, raw
- 4 tablespoons chia seeds
- 3/4 cup almond meal
- ½ cup coconut oil (melted)
- ½ cup honey or maple syrup
- ½ cup dried fruit – try raisins, cranberries, banana chips, mango

Directions

1. Line a cookie sheet with parchment paper.
2. In a large mixing bowl, combine the melted coconut oil and honey or maple syrup. Add in all other ingredient expect for the dried fruit. Mix well to combine and thoroughly coat all ingredients.
3. Spread mixture onto cookie sheet into thin layer. Bake in preheated 325 degree oven for 20 minutes, remove tray from oven and flip mixture over with spatula. Return to oven and cook for another 20 minutes or until it is golden brown.
4. Remove from oven and add sprinkle with dried fruit. Allow to cool. Can be stored in an airtight container for up to a week.

Banana Apple Smoothie with Greens

Whip up this colorful smoothie for a quick on-the-go breakfast.

Servings: 4

Ingredients

- 1 ripe banana
- 1 apple, cored and peeled
- 1 carrot, chopped
- 2 cups filtered water
- 1 tablespoon raw honey
- 1 cup whole coconut milk
- 4 cups greens—romaine, spinach, chard, kale, collards, parsley etc.

Directions

1. In a food processor, combine all ingredients except the greens. Process until smooth.

2. Mix in four cups of mixed greens and blend until smooth.

Zucchini and Red Pepper Shakshuka

Shakshuka means eggs poached in a spicy tomato and onion sauce.
This one-pan meal is perfect for breakfast or dinner.

Servings: 4

Ingredients

- 3 tablespoons olive oil
- 3 cloves garlic, minced
- 1 large yellow onion, sliced thin
- 1 large zucchini, cut into bite-size chunks
- 2 red peppers, diced
- 1 cup tomato sauce
- 2 bay leaves
- 1 teaspoon crushed red pepper
- ½ cup fresh cilantro, chopped
- Himalayan salt and freshly ground black pepper to taste
- 8 large eggs

Directions

1. Heat olive oil in large, heavy-duty skillet over medium-high heat. Add garlic and onions and sauté for 3-4 minutes until onions soften and turn translucent.

2. Lower heat to medium and add zucchini and peppers. Continue to sauté, stirring occasionally, for another 5 minutes or until vegetables are tender.

3. Add tomato sauce, bay leaves. crushed red pepper, cilantro, salt, and pepper to pan. Stir to mix.

4. Reduce heat to low. Make 8 wells in the pan to hold the eggs. Crack and egg gently into each well. Cover pan with lid and let simmer for 5 minutes.

5. Remove cover and check eggs. If whites are not set, recover pan, and cook for an additional 2-4 minutes, checking frequently, until whites are set.

6. Remove from heat and serve immediately.

Poultry Dishes

Chicken is so versatile it provides countless options for Paleo meals.

Paleo Teriyaki Wings

These moist, flavorful, wings can be on your table in about 30 minutes.

Servings: 4

Ingredients
- ½ cup coconut aminos
- ½ cup honey
- ¼ cup orange juice
- 2 tablespoons rice vinegar
- 1 teaspoon arrowroot flour
- 1 tablespoon fresh ginger, grated
- 2 cloves garlic, minced
- 1 tablespoon sesame oil
- 1 teaspoon red pepper flakes
- Coconut oil, for greasing pan
- 1 ½ pounds chicken wings
- Chopped green onions for garnish

Directions

1. Preheat oven to 425 degrees

2. Combine all ingredients through red pepper flakes in saucepan over medium heat. Bring to boil and then remove from heat. Allow to cool slightly.

3. Grease a baking dish with coconut oil.

4. Place chicken wings in large bowl. Reserve a ¼ cup of teriyaki sauce mixture and pour rest of sauce over chicken and mix until chicken is thoroughly coated on all sides. Place chicken wings in baking dish in single layer.

5. Bake in oven for 10 minutes. Remove chicken from oven, turn pieces over and baste with more teriyaki sauce. Return to oven and cook for another 10-15 minutes until chicken is cooked through (internal temperature should reach 165 degrees).

6. Remove from oven and brush with reserved teriyaki sauce. Garnish with green onions.

Cran-Apple Chicken Salad

This is a tasty way to use up leftover chicken.

Servings: 4

Ingredients

- 1 1/2 pounds chicken breast, cooked and diced
- 1/3 cup dried cranberries
- 1 cup celery, chopped
- 1/2 cup red onion, chopped
- 1 apple, cored and chopped
- 1/2 cup grapes, halved
- 1/2 cup walnuts, chopped
- 1/2 cup Paleo Mayonnaise
- 1 teaspoon lemon juice
- Salt and fresh ground pepper, to taste

Directions

1. In a bowl, combine chicken, cranberries, celery, red onion, apple, grapes, and walnuts.

2. Fold in mayonnaise, lemon, and salt and pepper. Mix until all ingredients are coated.

3. Serve at once or refrigerate.

Crunchy-Spicy Baked Chicken Drumsticks

These crunchy chicken legs are so easy to prepare yet so tasty they're sure to become a family favorite.

Servings: 4

Ingredients

- 12 chicken drumsticks
- 2 tablespoons olive oil or coconut oil
- 1/2 almond flour
- 1 teaspoon garlic powder
- 1 teaspoon paprika
- 1 teaspoon cayenne pepper
- Salt and freshly ground black pepper, to taste

Directions

1. Preheat oven to 400 degrees.

2. Using basting brush, coat chicken with olive oil or coconut oil.

3. In a large bowl, combine almond flour, garlic powder, paprika, cayenne pepper, salt, and pepper.

4. Add chicken to bowl and toss until chicken is covered with seasonings.

5. Arrange drumsticks on baking sheet. Cook for 30 minutes. Turn chicken over and continue cooking for another 30 minutes or until chicken is cooked through.

Crispy Coconut Chicken Fingers with Honey Mustard Sauce

These are so good you might want to make a double batch.

Servings: 3-4

Ingredients

- 1 pound chicken tenderloins
- 1 egg
- 1/2 cup almond flour
- 1 cup shredded coconut, unsweetened
- 1/2 teaspoon salt
- 2 tablespoons coconut oil
- Mustard Sauce, for dipping

Directions

1. Preheat oven to 350 degrees.
2. In a bowl, whisk the egg. In a separate bowl, combine almond flour, coconut, and salt.
3. Dip chicken strips into egg and then coat with almond-coconut mixture.
4. Heat a large skillet over medium-high heat. Add coconut oil to pan and let heat.
5. Add chicken strips to pan and cook until light browned on one side, about 3-4 minutes. Flip chicken over and cook another 4 minutes or until chicken is cooked all the way through.
6. Serve with Honey Mustard Sauce for dipping.

Curried Chicken Stew

This curry is spicy, which I love, but you can tone it down by cutting out the red chilies and it will still taste delicious. Although the ingredient list looks long, it is mostly spices, and this dish is quite easy to prepare.

Servings: 6

Ingredients

- 3 tablespoons ghee or coconut oil
- 2 medium yellow onions, chopped
- 1 tablespoon of fresh ginger, finely chopped
- 4 garlic cloves, minced
- 2 large carrots, chopped
- 2 1/2 pounds boneless, skinless chicken breast, cut into chunks
- 2 15-ounce cans coconut milk, unsweetened
- 2 cups chicken stock
- 2 tablespoons tomato paste
- 4 medium tomatoes, chopped
- 2 teaspoons cinnamon
- 1-2 red chilies
- 2 tablespoons curry powder
- 1/4 cup fresh cilantro, chopped
- Juice of 1 lemon
- Salt and freshly ground black pepper, to taste

Directions

1. In large pot, heat ghee or coconut oil over medium heat. Add onions, ginger, carrots, and garlic and cook until onions are soft, about 5 minutes. Add the chicken chunks and cook for another 3-4 minutes.
2. Add all remaining ingredients to pot and stir so tomato paste and spices are well blended. Bring to low simmer and then reduce heat to low.
3. Let simmer until chicken is cooked through, about 15-20 minutes.

Chicken Piccata

This classic dish is well-suited to the Paleo diet.

Servings: 4

Ingredients

- 1 ½ pounds chicken tenders, boneless, skinless
- 3 tablespoons coconut flour
- 5 tablespoons olive oil
- 3 lemons, freshly squeezed plus 5-6 slices
- 2 tablespoons fresh parsley, chopped
- 2 tablespoons capers, minced
- ½ cup green olives
- Sea salt and freshly ground black pepper, to taste

Directions

1. On a chopping board, pound the chicken parts using a kitchen mallet to flatten to ¼ inch thickness. Lightly coat with flour.

2. In a large pan, heat oil over medium-high heat and cook chicken for about 2 minutes per side or until just browned and cooked through. Add lemon juice, capers, olives, lemon slices, and parsley. Lower heat, and simmer for about 3-5 minutes. Sprinkle with salt and pepper to taste.

Grilled Chicken Salad with Mango and Avocado

This makes a nice light supper on a summer night.

Servings: 4

Ingredients

- 2 tablespoons olive oil, divided
- Juice of 1 lime
- 1 tablespoon honey
- 1 teaspoon fresh ginger, grated
- 4 skinless, boneless chicken breasts
- 2 mangoes, peeled and diced
- 2 avocadoes, peeled and diced
- 8 cups mixed salad greens
- 1 tablespoon balsamic vinegar

Directions

1. In a small bowl, combine 1 tablespoon olive oil, lime, honey, and ginger.

2. Place chicken on plate and brush each side with oil mixture.

3. Grill chicken until cooked through, flipping once and brushing with oil mixture. Slice cooked chicken into strips.

4. Add salad greens to large salad bowl. Add sliced chicken, mango, and avocado. Drizzle with remaining olive oil and balsamic vinegar.

Bun-less Paleo Turkey Burgers

These burgers are so juicy and delicious that you won't miss the bun.

Servings: 4

Ingredients

- 1 pound ground turkey
- 1/4 small onion, finely diced
- 1 egg white, lightly beaten
- 1 clove garlic, minced
- 1 tablespoon fresh parsley, finely chopped
- Salt and freshly ground black pepper, to taste

Directions

1. In a large bowl, mix turkey and all other ingredients. Form into 4 patties.

2. Cook the patties in a skillet over medium heat until cooked through, turning once during cooking (about 5-6 minutes per side). Could also be cooked on the grill.

3. Serve topped with your favorite burger toppings: caramelized onions, sautéed mushroom, avocado slices, etc. Wrap in large romaine leaf in place of bun.

Asian Chicken Lettuce Wraps

These are addictively good!

Servings: 4

Ingredients

- 1 tablespoon coconut oil
- 1 pound ground chicken
- 2 cloves garlic, minced
- 1 medium yellow onion, diced
- ¼ cup coconut aminos
- 2 tablespoons rice wine vinegar
- 1 tablespoon freshly grated ginger
- 1 teaspoon Sriracha hot chili sauce, or more to taste
- 1 can (8-ounce) sliced water chestnuts, drained
- 2 green onions, sliced thin
- Sea salt and freshly ground black pepper to taste
- 1 head butter lettuce

Directions

1. Heat olive oil in large skillet over medium-high heat. Add ground chicken and cook, stirring, until chicken is browned, about 4-5 minutes. Drain.
2. Add garlic, onion, coconut aminos, rice wine vinegar, ginger, and Sriracha and cook for another 2-3 minutes or until onions are translucent. Add water chestnuts and green onions and cook for another 2-3 minutes. Season with salt and pepper, to taste.
3. Serve by spooning a couple of tablespoons into the center of a lettuce leaf.
4.

Honey Orange Chicken

This is better than the Chinese takeout version! Serve with Cauli-Rice.

Servings: 4

Ingredients

- 2 tablespoons coconut oil
- 1 1/2 pounds chicken breast, cubed
- 4 garlic cloves, minced
- 4 tablespoons fresh ginger, grated
- 4 tablespoons coconut aminos
- 3 tablespoons honey
- 2 tablespoons chili sauce
- 2 tablespoons fish sauce
- 1/2 cup orange juice
- 2 scallions, chopped

Directions

1. Heat coconut oil in large skillet over medium-high heat. Add chicken pieces and stir-fry until chicken starts to brown.

2. Add in garlic and ginger and stir-fry an additional 1-2 minutes.

3. Lower heat to medium-low and add in coconut aminos, honey, chili sauce, fish sauce, and orange juice. Stir together and then let simmer, uncovered for 10 minutes or until chicken is cooked through and sauce has thickened.

4. Serve topped with chopped scallions.

Teriyaki Chicken Stir-Fry

This only takes about 15 minutes to cook so you can have dinner ready in no time.

Servings: 4

Ingredients

- 2 tablespoons coconut oil
- 1 medium onion, chopped
- 2 cloves garlic, minced
- 4 boneless, skinless chicken breast, cut into small pieces
- 2 large carrots, peeled and sliced thin
- 1 red pepper, sliced thin
- 2 cups broccoli florets, cut into small pieced
- 1 can water chestnuts, drained

Sauce

- 1/3 cup coconut aminos
- 1/4 cup honey
- 2 tablespoons rice wine vinegar
- 2 teaspoons arrowroot flour

Directions

1. Heat coconut oil in a large skillet or wok over medium-high heat. Add the onion and garlic and cook for 2-3 minutes until onion starts to soften. Add the chicken and cook, stirring occasionally, until chicken starts to brown, about 3-4 minutes. Add carrots, red pepper, broccoli, and water chestnuts, and continue cooking until vegetables soften, about 3-4 minutes.

2. In a small bowl, whisk together sauce ingredients. Pour over chicken and vegetables. Continue cooking and stirring until chicken and vegetables are coated with sauce.

3. Serve immediately.

Paleo Chicken and Mushrooms

This is a Paleo version of the classic chicken Marsala.

Servings: 4

Ingredients
- ½ cup almond flour
- 1 teaspoon thyme
- 1 teaspoon garlic powder
- ½ teaspoon oregano
- ½ teaspoon cayenne pepper
- 1/1 teaspoon sea salt
- ½ teaspoon freshly ground black pepper
- 2 (6-8 ounce) boneless, skinless chicken breast, cut into bite-size chunks
- 1 tablespoon olive oil
- 3 tablespoons ghee
- 3 cups baby mushrooms, stems trimmed
- 1 medium yellow onion, sliced thin
- 8-10 grape tomatoes
- 1 ½ cups chicken stock

Directions

1. In a bowl, mix together the almond flour, spices, salt, and pepper. Dredge chicken pieces in the flour mixture. Shake to remove excess and place on plate.

2. In a large skillet, heat olive oil and 1 tablespoon of ghee over medium-high heat. Add chicken pieces and cook until chicken is golden brown on all sides, about 5-6 minutes. Remove chicken from pan and set aside.

3. Add another tablespoon of ghee to pan and add mushrooms and onions. Cook, stirring frequently, until mushrooms have softened and onions are translucent, about 4-5 minutes. Add tomatoes and cook for an additional 1-2 minutes.

4. Add chicken stock to pan as well as chicken pieces and remaining tablespoon of ghee. Continue to cook, stirring often, until chicken has cooked through and sauce has thickened, about 4-5 minutes. Add additional salt and pepper to taste. Serve immediately.

Ground Turkey and Sweet Potato Casserole

This is a delicious, filling casserole that should satisfy even the heartiest appetites.

Servings: 6-8

Ingredients

- 2 tablespoons olive oil
- 1 large yellow onion, diced
- 2 cloves garlic, minced
- 1 red pepper, diced
- 2 pounds ground turkey meat
- 2 teaspoons cayenne pepper
- 1 teaspoon dried oregano
- 1 teaspoon paprika
- 1 teaspoon cinnamon
- Salt and freshly ground black pepper, to taste
- 4 eggs
- 2-3 large sweet potatoes, peeled and sliced thin

Directions

1. In a large skillet, heat olive oil over medium-high heat. Add onion, garlic, and red pepper and sauté for 2-3 minutes until onion and pepper start to soften. Add ground turkey and spices. Cook, stirring occasionally, until turkey is browned.

2. Meanwhile, whisk eggs in a bowl.

3. In a large casserole pan, spread a layer of sliced sweet potatoes. Next, add layer of turkey mixture. Repeat layers. Pour beaten eggs over casserole and top with final layer of sweet potatoes.

4. Baked in preheated 350 degree oven for 45-50 minutes or until sweet potatoes are soft.

Turkey Pumpkin Chili

This is a perfect way to use up leftover turkey meat and can be whipped up in about 15 minutes.

Servings: 4

Ingredients

- 4 cups roasted turkey meat, cubed
- 1 large yellow onion, diced
- 1 green pepper, diced
- 1 stalk celery, diced
- 1 tablespoon olive oil
- 1 1/2 cups pumpkin puree
- 1 pint-size jar crushed tomatoes
- 2 tablespoons ancho chili powder
- 2 teaspoons ground cumin
- 1 teaspoon oregano
- 1 teaspoon garlic powder
- Salt and freshly ground black pepper, to taste

Directions

1. In a large pan, heat oil over medium heat. Mix in onion, green pepper and celery; cook until tender, about 3-4 minutes. Sprinkle salt and pepper to taste. Mix in the spices and cook for another minute until fragrant. Add pumpkin, tomatoes, and turkey meat and simmer for another 10 minutes.

2. Serve hot.

Meat Dishes (Beef, Pork, and Lamb)

Opt for grass-fed organic beef if at all possible. This is available at most supermarkets now and is well-worth the extra cost.

Paleo Chili

This beanless chili has a rich smoky flavor. This could also be made in a slow cooker to let the flavors meld together.

Servings: 6

Ingredients

- 1 tablespoon coconut oil
- 1 large yellow onion, chopped
- 1 large green bell pepper, chopped
- 1 large red bell pepper, chopped
- 6 garlic cloves, minced
- 1 1/2 pounds ground beef
- 1 pound ground pork
- 2 tablespoons chili powder
- 1 tablespoon cumin
- 2 teaspoons dried oregano
- 2 teaspoons cayenne pepper
- 1 teaspoon cocoa powder, unsweetened
- 2 teaspoons Worcestershire sauce
- 1 can (28 ounces) crushed tomatoes
- 2 tablespoons tomato paste
- Salt and freshly ground black pepper, to taste

Directions

1. Heat coconut oil in large pot over medium heat. Add onions, bell peppers, and garlic and sauté until vegetables are tender, about 7-9 minutes.

2. Add ground beef and pork to pot and continue cooking and stirring until meat is browned, 7-8 minutes.

3. Add spices and all remaining ingredients to pot. Stir, reduce heat to low and simmer for 25-30 minutes.

Portobello Burger

Using Portobello mushroom caps in place of the bun is a great twist on the traditional burger.

Servings: 4 burgers

Ingredients

- 8 Portobello mushrooms,
- 2 tablespoons olive oil
- 2 tablespoons ghee
- 3 tablespoons balsamic vinegar
- 1 pound ground beef
- 1/2 medium yellow onion, minced
- 1 tablespoon Dijon mustard
- Salt and freshly ground black pepper, to taste
- Toppings: lettuce, tomato, red onions, your favorite

Directions

1. Remove stems from mushrooms. Wash caps and pat dry.

2. Add butter and olive oil to large skillet over medium heat. Add mushrooms and cook for 4-5 minutes. Flip mushrooms over cook for an addition 3-4 minutes. Remove from pan to plate. Sprinkle caps with salt and pepper and drizzle a little vinegar over each one.

3. In a bowl, combine ground beef with minced onion and mustard. Add salt and pepper. Form into 4 patties, about half-inch thick.

4. Cook burgers, either in skillet or on grill. Cook to desired doneness, flipping burgers once during cooking.

5. Place burger on mushroom cap, top with lettuce, tomato, onions, or desired toppings. Top with another Portobello mushroom cap.

Slow Cooker Beef Ragu with Zoodles

The prep time for this is quick, but let the meat slow-cook for hours for a rich, deep flavor.

Servings: 4

Ingredients

- 2 tablespoons olive oil
- 1/2 yellow onion, finely chopped
- 2 celery sticks, chopped
- 2 medium carrots, peeled and chopped
- 1 1/2 pounds ground beef, preferably grass-fed
- 2 large cans whole peeled tomatoes
- 1 cup beef stock
- 1/2 cup water
- 1/3 cup balsamic vinegar
- 1 recipe Zoodles

Directions

1. Heat oil in large skillet over medium-high heat. Add onion and sauté for 1-2 minutes. Add celery and carrots and continue cooking for an additional 1-2 minutes. Add ground beef to pan and cook, stirring until beef is browned. Remove pan from heat.

2. Add ground beef mixture to slow cooker. Add peeled tomatoes, beef stock, water, and balsamic vinegar. Turn slow cooker to high, and let simmer for 3-4 hours.

3. Serve over Zoodles.

Beef and Veggie Stir Fry with Ginger-Orange Sauce

This stir fry cooks up in just 10 minutes (plus prep time) and has a delicious orange-ginger sauce.

Servings: 4

Ingredients

Marinade:
- 1/2 cup orange juice
- 4 tablespoons coconut aminos
- 2 teaspoons sesame oil
- 2 teaspoons fresh grated ginger
- 3 garlic cloves, minced

Stir Fry:
- 1 tablespoon coconut oil
- 1 pound flank steak, sliced into thin strips
- 1 small yellow onion, diced
- 1 red bell pepper, sliced thin
- 3 stalks celery, chopped
- 1 large carrot, cut into julienne slices
- 1 small bunch broccoli, cut into small florets
- Diced green onions, for garnish

Directions

1. Combine marinade ingredients in large bowl. Add steak strips and mix so steak is fully coated in marinade. Cover and refrigerate for 30 minutes.

2. Heat coconut oil in large skillet or wok over high heat. Add onion and stir fry for 1-2 minutes.

3. Remove beef from refrigerator, and drain, reserving the marinade. Add to beef to pan and stir fry for 2-3 minutes. Add onion, bell pepper, celery, carrot, broccoli, and marinade to pan. Continue cooking, stirring frequently, until veggies are tender and marinade starts to thicken.

4. Remove from heat. Top with diced green onion for garnish. Serve over bed of Cauli-rice.

Beef Stew with Butternut Squash

This aromatic stew with just a hint of sweetness is perfect for a crisp autumn day.

Servings: 4

Ingredients

- 3 tablespoons olive oil
- 1 medium yellow onion, diced
- 3 cloves garlic, minced
- 2 pounds stew beef, cut into cubes
- 1 can (16 ounces) diced tomatoes
- 1 large butternut squash, trimmed and cut into bite-size cubes
- 4 cups beef broth
- 1 tablespoon rosemary
- 1 tablespoon thyme
- Salt and freshly ground black pepper, to taste

Directions

1. Heat olive oil in large pot over medium heat. Add onions and garlic and sauté for 2-3 minutes. Add the beef cubes and cook until the beef is browned, about 5 minutes.

2. Add the diced tomatoes, butternut squash, beef broth, rosemary, and thyme. Turn heat to high and bring to a boil, then reduce heat to low and let simmer, covered, for an hour. Add salt and freshly ground black pepper to taste.

Yummy Homestyle Meatloaf

Comfort food at its best.

Servings: 4-6

Ingredients
- 1 tablespoon olive oil
- 1 large yellow onion, diced
- 3 garlic cloves, minced
- 1 pound ground beef
- 1 pound ground pork
- 2 tablespoons tomato paste
- 1/2 cup almond flour
- 2 large eggs
- 1 tablespoon oregano
- Salt and freshly ground black pepper, to taste
- 1 can (8 ounce) tomato sauce

Directions

1. In a medium pan, heat olive oil over medium-high heat. Add onion and garlic and sauté for 3-4 minutes. remove from heat and set aside.

2. In a large bowl, combine ground beef, ground pork, onion mixture, tomato paste, almond flour, eggs, oregano, salt, and pepper. Mix together with fork.

3. Brush shallow baking dish with olive oil. Place ground meat mixture in center of pan and form into loaf shape. Spread tomato sauce on top.

4. Bake in preheated 400 degree oven for 45 minutes or until meat loaf is cooked through and internal temperature reaches 160 degrees.

5. Serve with mashed cauliflower.

Roasted Pepper Stuffed with Spinach, Walnuts, and Ground Beef

These scrumptious stuffed peppers have just a hint of cinnamon.

Servings: 4

Ingredients
- 2 tablespoons olive oil
- 1 medium yellow onion, diced
- 3 cloves garlic, minced
- 1 pound ground beef
- 2 cups baby spinach, chopped
- 2 eggs
- 1/2 cup walnuts, chopped
- 1 1/2 tablespoons cinnamon
- 1 tablespoon cardamom
- Salt and freshly ground black pepper, to taste
- 8 large bell peppers
- Parsley, for garnish

Directions

1. Heat olive oil in large pan over medium heat. Add onion and garlic and sauté for 2-3 minutes, until onion starts to soften. Add ground beef and continue to cook until beef is browned, about 5-6 minutes. Add baby spinach and sauté 2-3 more minutes, until spinach has wilted.

2. Remove from heat and place beef mixture into large bowl. Crack in eggs and add walnuts, cinnamon, cardamom, salt and pepper. Mix together all ingredients.

3. Cut tops of peppers and remove seeds. Place peppers in large shallow baking dish. Fill each pepper with 1/8 of ground beef mixture.

4. Cook in preheated 350 degree oven for 45 minutes. Garnish with parsley.

5.

Beef and Veggie Kebabs with Spicy Mediterranean Marinade

The spicy marinade gives the meat and veggies a nice kick.

Servings: 4

Ingredients

Marinade

- 1/3 cup olive oil
- 2 tablespoons tomato paste
- 5 cloves garlic, minced
- 1 tablespoon lemon juice
- 1 tablespoon honey
- 1 teaspoon salt
- 1/2 teaspoon cumin
- 1/2 teaspoon paprika
- 1/2 teaspoon coriander
- 1/2 teaspoon freshly ground pepper

Kebabs

- 1 1/2 pounds sirloin, cut into 1-inch cubes
- 1/2 pound mushrooms, stems trimmed
- 1 large summer squash, cut into 1-inch chunks

- 1 medium red onion, cut into 1-inch chunks
- 1 bell pepper, cut into 1-inch chunks
- 1 carton grape tomatoes
- 10 (12-inch) skewers (if using wooden skewers, soak in water for 30 minutes before using)

Directions

1. In a large bowl, whisk together all of the ingredients for the marinade. Put 1/4 cup of the marinade into a large zip lock bag. Add the beef cubes to the bag, seal it, and shake bag to thoroughly coat beef with marinade. Set aside and allow beef to marinate for at least thirty minutes.

2. Add the vegetables to the bowl with marinade. Stir to coat the vegetables with marinade. Thread the vegetables onto 6 skewers, alternating between type of vegetables. Allow a little space between each piece.

3. When beef is ready, thread onto 4 skewers, leaving a little space between each piece.

4. Place all of the skewers onto a hot grill. Close grill cover and cook, turning skewers every couple of minutes. Remove beef skewers when they are at your desired doneness, about 6-8 minutes for medium rare, 8-10 minutes for medium, and 10-12 minutes for medium well. Transfer to serving platter and cover with foil.

5. Continue cooking vegetable skewers until vegetables are lightly charred and tender. Add to serving platter with beef kebabs. Serve immediately.

Slow Cooker Short Ribs

This recipe only takes 10 minutes of hands-on time.

Servings: 4

Ingredients

- 1 tablespoon coconut oil
- 2 pounds beef short ribs, grass-fed
- Salt and freshly ground black pepper, to taste
- 3 tablespoons balsamic vinegar
- 1 tablespoon Dijon mustard
- 1/2 cup water

Directions

1. Heat coconut oil in heavy skillet over medium-high heat until oil is hot. Add the ribs and sear on all sides. Season with salt and pepper.

2. Transfer ribs to slow cooker.

3. In a small bowl, whisk together vinegar, mustard, and water. Pour over ribs.

4. Set slow cooker to low and let cook for eight hours.

5. Serve with steamed veggies.

Grilled Steak with Ginger Marinade

This recipe is very simple, but oh so delicious.

Servings: 4

Ingredients

- 1 piece of fresh ginger (about 6-inches), sliced into thin slices
- 1/4 cup sesame oil
- 8 cloves garlic, minced
- 2 teaspoons lemon juice
- 1 tablespoon honey
- 2 teaspoons salt
- 1 teaspoon freshly ground pepper
- 1 1/2 pounds flank steak, trimmed
- 1 tablespoon coconut oil

Directions

1. In a bowl, whisk together all ingredients except steak. Pour into large resealable plastic bag. Add flank steak, seal, and shake to thoroughly coat steak with marinade.

2. Allow to marinade for 30 minutes at room temperature. Can also marinate in refrigerator for up to 24 hours.

3. Heat coconut oil in large grill pan over medium-high heat.

4. Remove steak from marinade, allow excess marinade to drip off. Add to pan and cook to desired doneness, about 6-8 minutes per side for medium rare, 8-10 minutes for medium, and 10-12 minutes for medium well.

5. Remove from pan and place on cutting board and let rest for 5-10 minutes. Slice, against the grain, into thin slices. Serve.

Asian-Style Short Ribs

Although you'll need to plan ahead to marinate these ribs, the hands-on cooking time is very brief.

Servings: 8

Ingredients
- 3 pounds beef short ribs, cut across the bone
- 1 pear, grated
- 1 lime, juiced
- ½ inch ginger, peeled and grated
- 2 tablespoons sesame seeds
- 1 cup soda water
- 1 cup coconut aminos
- 1/4 cup sesame oil
- 1/4 cup honey
- 6 cloves garlic, minced

Directions

1. In a bowl, combine all ingredients except the ribs. Mix until well blended. Put the ribs into a large resealable plastic bag (gallon size) and add the marinade. Massage bag to mix and marinate in refrigerator at least 4 hours or overnight.

2. Take meat from the fridge and allow to come to room temperature (about 30 minutes). Preheat a grill at high heat. Lightly grease its grates. Cook ribs for about 3 minutes per side.

Beef and Broccoli Fried Cauli-Rice

Better, and healthier, than Chinese take-out fried rice.

Servings: 4

Ingredients

- 1 head cauliflower
- 3 tablespoons coconut oil, divided
- 1 medium yellow onion, diced
- 2 celery sticks, chopped
- 1 red bell pepper, sliced thin
- 1/2 cup mushrooms, sliced
- 2 cups broccoli florets, cut small
- 1 can water chestnuts, drained
- 1 pound beef sirloin, sliced into 1-inch cubes
- 1/2 teaspoon salt
- 1 teaspoon freshly ground black pepper
- 1/2 teaspoon Chinese five spice
- 1 small piece ginger (1-inch), grated
- 2 small chili peppers, finely chopped
- 1/4 cup coconut aminos
- 2 tablespoons rice vinegar

- 1 tablespoon fish sauce
- 2 eggs, whisked

Directions

1. Cut the cauliflower into small florets and place into food processor. Pulse until it has the texture of rice. This can also be done using a box grater.

2. Heat 2 tablespoons of coconut oil in a large skillet or wok over high heat. Add the onions, celery, and bell pepper and stir-fry for 2-3 minutes until onion begin to soften. Add mushrooms and broccoli and stir-fry for another 2-3 minutes, or until broccoli begins to soften.

3. Add another tablespoon of coconut oil and the beef sirloin to the pan. Sprinkle with salt and pepper and continue to stir-fry until beef is browned on all sides.

4. Add in Chinese five spice, grated ginger, chili peppers, coconut aminos, rice vinegar, and fish sauce. Stir until well blended and continue to cook, stirring often, until beef is cooked through.

5. Lower heat to medium and add in cauliflower. Continue to stir-fry another 3-4 minutes until cauliflower starts to soften. Pour in whisked eggs and stir-fry another 1-2 minutes until eggs are cooked. Serve immediately.

Slow-Cooked Pork Carnitas

The slow-cooked pork is melt-in-your-mouth tender.

Servings: 6

Ingredients

- 1 teaspoon cumin
- 1 teaspoon coriander
- 1 teaspoon salt
- 1 teaspoon freshly ground black pepper
- 1 teaspoon oregano
- 1 teaspoon garlic powder
- 1 teaspoon cinnamon
- 2 1/2-3 pound pork shoulder
- I tablespoon olive oil
- 1 medium Vivaldi onion, chopped
- 1 can green chilies
- 1 cup beef stock
- 1 bay leaf

Directions

1. In a bowl, combine first seven ingredients (through cinnamon). Rub this mixture all over pork shoulder coating all sides thoroughly.

2. Put on olive oil and onion into bottom of slow cooker. Place pork shoulder into slow cooker. Add green chilies, beef stock and bay leaf. Cover and cook on low for 8-10 hours until pork comes apart easily with fork. Alternatively, cook on high for 4 hours and then turn down to low for additional 2-3 hours. Add additional salt and pepper to taste. Shred pork into bite-sized pieces.

3. Serve on top of bed of romaine lettuce and top with any (or all) of the following: guacamole, salsa, chopped tomato, chopped red onion, shredded cheese (if you eat dairy).

Spanish Chorizo Stew with Sweet Potatoes and Kale

This spicy stew is perfect for a quick and delicious dinner.

Servings: 6

Ingredients
- 2 tablespoons olive oil
- 1 medium Vivaldi onion, diced
- 3 garlic cloves, minced
- 1/2 pound chorizo sausage, cut into 1/2 inch pieces
- 3 celery stalks, diced
- 3 large carrots, peeled and diced
- 2 teaspoons cumin
- 2 teaspoons paprika
- 1 teaspoon tumeric
- 1 large pinch saffron
- 2 sweet potatoes, peeled and cut into 1-inch cubes
- 8 cups chicken broth, homemade or low-sodium
- 4 cups kale, cut into small pieces
- 1 can (8-ounce) diced tomatoes
- 1 lemon, juiced
- Salt and freshly ground black pepper, to taste

Directions

1. Heat olive oil in a large pot over medium-high heat. Add onions and garlic and sauté for 3-4 minutes, until onions are translucent. Add sausage and continue cooking for an additional 3-4 minutes.

2. Add celery and carrots, and continue cooking, stirring frequently, another 3-4 minutes. Add remaining ingredients through diced tomatoes to pot, bring to a boil, reduce heat to low, and simmer until sweet potatoes are tender, about 30 minutes.

3. Add lemon juice, salt, and pepper. Serve hot.

Glazed Pork Chops with Apricot-Mango Salsa

These pork chops are so easy to prepare and mouth-wateringly good.

Servings: 4

Ingredients
- 1/3 cup Dijon mustard
- 3 tablespoons balsamic vinegar
- 1 teaspoon cumin
- Salt and fresh ground black pepper, to taste
- 4 pork chops

For the Apricot-Mango Salsa

- 4 fresh apricots, pit removed, diced
- 1 ripe mango, peeled, diced
- 1/4 red onion, diced small
- 1/4 cup fresh basil, minced
- 1/4 cup extra virgin olive oil
- 1 teaspoon cardamom

Directions

1. In a bowl, mix mustard, vinegar, and cumin.

2. Sprinkle both sides of pork chops with salt and pepper. Brush mustard mixture onto pork chops, covering both sides.

3. Grill pork chops over medium-high heat for about 5 minutes per side. Baste with mustard sauce when they're flipped. They could also be broiled in the oven, flipping once.

4. While pork chops are cooking, mix together ingredients for relish in a bowl.

5. When pork chops are finished, top with salsa.

Slow-Cooker Pork Chili Verde

Let the slow cooker do the work for this melt-in-your-mouth, spicy dish.

Servings: 6

Ingredients

- 2 tablespoons olive oil
- 2 1/2 pound pork shoulder, cut into 1-inch cubes
- 1 pound tomatillos, husk removed, diced
- 1 can (6 ounces) Hatch green chilies
- 1 large yellow onion, diced
- 6 garlic cloves, minced
- 2 cups beef stock
- 1 tablespoon cumin
- 1 tablespoon oregano
- 1 tablespoon coriander
- 1/2 cup fresh cilantro, minced
- Salt and freshly ground black pepper, to taste

Directions

1. Heat olive oil in a large skillet over medium-high heat. Add pork cubes and brown on all sides, about 4-5 minutes. Remove pork and set aside.

2. Lower heat to medium and add the tomatillos, chilies, onion, and garlic. Sauté for 4-5 minutes or until onions start to soften. Remove from heat and transfer to slow cooker.

3. Add pork, beef stock, cumin, oregano, coriander, cilantro, salt, and pepper to slow cooker. Cover and cook on low for 6-7 hours or until pork is tender.

Paleo Breakfast Sausage

This breakfast treat is packed with spices that are full of ant-inflammatory compounds.

Servings: Makes 8 patties

Ingredients

- 1 pound ground lean pork
- 2 teaspoons fresh sage leaves, finely chopped
- 1 teaspoons. fresh thyme, finely chopped
- 3/4 teaspoon ground black pepper
- 1/4 teaspoon ground nutmeg
- 1/4 teaspoon cayenne pepper
- 1/4 teaspoon fresh rosemary, chopped
- 1/4 teaspoon red pepper flakes
- 1 tablespoon olive oil

Directions

1. In a large bowl, combine all ingredients. Manually mix until well blended. Form 8 patties.

2. In a medium non-stick pan heat oil over medium heat. Cook patties in batches for about 9 minutes on one side then another 6 minutes on the other side or until well browned.

Greek-Style Lamb Meatballs

Serve these tasty meatball with a big Greek salad for a quick meal.

Servings: 4

Ingredients

- 1 1/2 pounds ground lamb
- 2 cloves garlic
- 1 teaspoon oregano
- 1/2 teaspoon garlic powder
- Salt and freshly ground black pepper, to taste
- Zest of 1 lemon
- 2 tablespoons olive oil

Directions

1. In a large bowl, combine ground lamb, garlic, oregano, garlic powder, salt, pepper, and lemon zest.

2. Form meat mixture into about 16-20 meatballs.

3. Heat the olive oil in a large heavy-duty skillet over medium-high heat. Add the meatballs (this may need to be done in two batches) and cook, turning occasionally, until meatballs are cooked through or just slightly pink in the middle, about 12-15 minutes.

Easy, Tasty Lamb Chops

These lamb chops can be made start to finish in less than half hour.

Servings: 4

Ingredients

- 2 garlic cloves, crushed
- 1 tablespoon rosemary, crushed
- 1 teaspoon thyme
- 2 tablespoons Dijon mustard
- 2 tablespoons lemon juice plus additional slices for garnish
- 3 tablespoons olive oil
- 1 tablespoon ghee
- 4 lamb chops (about 1-inch thick)
- Salt and freshly ground black pepper, to taste

Directions

1. In a bowl, combine garlic, rosemary, thyme, mustard, lemon juice, and 1 tablespoon of the olive oil. Stir until well blended. Spread mixture over lamb chops, coating both sides thoroughly. Let marinate for 20 minutes at room temperature.

2. Heat remaining olive oil and ghee in a large heavy skillet or grill pan over high heat. When pan is very hot, add lamb chops and sear for 2-3 minutes. Flip chops over and cook for an additional 3-4 minutes or until desired level of doneness. Serve garnished with lemon slices.

Seafood Dishes

Cold-water fatty fish like salmon are a great source of omega-3 fatty acids.

Italian-Style Tuna Stuffed Peppers

These work great for both a light lunch or party appetizers.

Servings: About 24 stuffed peppers

Ingredients

- 2 16-ounce jars of mild or sweet cherry peppers
- 1 can tuna fish, drained
- 1 tablespoon lemon juice
- 1 tablespoon extra-virgin olive oil
- 1 tablespoon capers
- ½ cucumber, peeled and diced
- 1 pack roma tomatoes, red and yellow mixed, diced
- ½ red onion, diced
- ¼ cup balsamic vinegar
- Freshly ground black pepper, to taste

Directions

1. Drain peppers and pick out about 24 whole peppers. Cut off pepper stems and discard. With a small spoon, scoop out seeds. Rinse peppers and drain.

2. In a bowl, combine tuna, lemon juice, olive oil, capers, cucumber, tomatoes, and red onion.

3. Fill each pepper with tuna mixture and place on plate. Drizzle peppers with balsamic vinegar and sprinkle with pepper.

Citrus Baked Salmon

Serve on a plate of steamed fresh baby spinach.

Servings: 4

Ingredients

- 4 slices lemon
- 4 slices orange
- 4 salmon fillets (6-8 ounces each)
- Salt and freshly ground black pepper
- 2 tablespoons fresh dill, chopped
- 2 tablespoons sun-dried tomatoes
- 1 tablespoon olive oil
- 2/3 cup rice wine vinegar

Directions

1. Place lemon and orange slices, side by side, in the bottom of a large shallow baking dish. Place each salmon fillet across the citrus slices. Sprinkle with salt and pepper.

2. In a small bowl, combine dill, sun-dried tomatoes, olive oil, and rice wine vinegar. Drizzle mixture over salmon fillets.

3. Bake in preheated 400 degree oven for about 20 minutes or until salmon is cooked through.

Pecan-Crusted Fish with Orange Salsa

The crunchiness of the pecans combined with the orange salsa make for a very tasty dish.

Servings: 2

Ingredients

For the fish
- 1 cup pecans
- ¼ cup unsweetened coconut, shredded
- ½ teaspoon dried parsley
- ½ teaspoon dried tarragon
- ½ teaspoon dried thyme
- salt and pepper, to taste
- 2 fish filets (tilapia, mahi-mahi or cod)
- 1 egg white, beaten, in shallow bowl
- 2 tablespoon coconut oil

For the salsa
- 4 oranges, peeled and cut in halves
- ½ jalapeno peppers, seeds removed and finely diced
- ½ lime, juiced
- ½ small red onion, diced
- ½ lemon, juiced
- 2 tablespoon fresh cilantro, chopped
- pinch of salt

Directions

1. In a food processor, combine pecans and coconut; pulse until crumbly. Add seasonings and salt and pepper, pulse some more until fully blended. Place into a shallow bowl, alongside the bowl of beaten egg white.

2. In a skillet, heat oil over medium heat. Dip fish fillet into the egg white, then dredge into pecan mixture; fry for about 3 minutes per side or until golden brown.

3. Meanwhile prepare the salsa. Combine all ingredients into a bowl; mix well to blend. Serve fish topped with the salsa.

Mediterranean Cod

This dish is quick to make and packed with flavor.

Servings: 4

- 4 cod fillets (6-8 ounces each)
- Salt and freshly ground black pepper, to taste
- 3 tablespoons olive oil
- ¼ red onion, sliced thin
- 4 plum tomatoes, chopped
- 1/3 cup Kalamata olives, chopped
- 1 teaspoon thyme
- 1 teaspoon basil

Directions

1. Season cod fillets with salt and pepper.

2. Heat 2 tablespoons olive oil in large skillet over medium high heat. Add onion and cod fillets. Cook for 1-2 minutes, turn fish over.

3. Add tomatoes, olive, thyme, and basil. Reduce heat to medium, cover pan, and continue cooking for 2-3 minutes.

4. Drizzle remaining olive oil over cod, and continue to cook for an additional 2-3 minutes or until fish is cooked through and flakes easily with fork.

Shrimp and Avocado Ceviche

This is a fresh, spicy, summery salad.

Servings: 4

Ingredients

- 2 pounds cooked shrimp, peeled and chopped
- ¾ cup fresh lime juice
- 5 plum tomatoes, diced
- 1 small red onion, chopped
- ½ cup fresh cilantro, chopped
- 1 avocado, peeled, pitted, and diced
- 1 tablespoon Sriracha hot chili sauce
- Sea salt and freshly ground black pepper, to taste

Directions

1. Place shrimp, lime juice, tomatoes, and red onion in a bowl. Mix well to coat everything in lime juice. Cover and refrigerate for about an hour.

2. Remove from refrigerator and add fresh cilantro, avocado, chili sauce, salt and pepper. Mix to combine.

Lemony Garlic Shrimp over Zoodles

The flavors of garlic and lemon mingle in this light yet satisfying dish.

Servings: 2

Ingredients

- 12 large shrimp, peeled, deveined, tails intact
- 2 garlic cloves, crushed
- 2 tablespoons olive oil
- 1/4 teaspoon red pepper flakes
- 1 tablespoon fresh parsley, chopped
- 2 teaspoons lemon juice
- 1 teaspoon lemon zest
- 1 recipe Zoodles

Directions

1. In a large pan, heat oil over medium high heat. Sauté garlic and red pepper flakes for a few seconds then stir in shrimp. Cook for about 3 minutes or until shrimp starts to turn pink.

2. Mix in chopped parsley, lemon zest, and juice. Toss to blend.

3. Serve over Zoodles.

Healthy, Yummy, Real Tuna Salad

Tuna contains an abundant antioxidant compound known as selenoneine. This tuna salad offers this anti-inflammatory benefits in a delicious way.

Servings: 6

Ingredients

- 3 (6 ounce) cans tuna in water
- 1/8 cup celery (chopped)
- 5 teaspoons fresh dill (chopped)
- 1/4 cup red onion (chopped)
- 2 teaspoons mixed sprouts (chopped)
- 1 teaspoon mustard powder
- 3 teaspoons Paleo Mayonnaise
- 2 teaspoons Dijon mustard
- 1 dash onion powder
- 1 dash garlic and herb seasoning (prepared)
- Lettuce boats for serving

Directions

1. Drain tuna. In a salad bowl, combine tuna with celery, dill, red onion and sprouts. Mix thoroughly using a fork until a paste-like consistency is achieved.

2. Mix in powdered and Dijon mustards, until well blended. Adjust seasonings, as desired.

3. Stir in onion powder and garlic powder. Add mayonnaise, mix to totally blend.

4. Serve in lettuce leaf boats.

Crab and Spinach-Stuffed Mushrooms

These stuffed mushrooms are filling enough for a light dinner. Serve with a green salad.

Servings: 4

Ingredients

- 2 cups crab meat
- 10 ounce package frozen spinach, chopped, drained
- 1 1/2 pounds Portobello mushrooms, stems chopped, tops reserved
- 1/4 cup onions, chopped
- 2 cloves garlic, minced
- 1/2 teaspoon dried basil, crushed
- 1/2 dried oregano, crushed
- 1/4 teaspoon ground ginger
- 1/4 cup white wine vinegar
- 1 tablespoon fresh squeezed lemon juice

Directions

1. Preheat oven to 425 °F.

2. Ina non-stick pan, cook mushroom stems, onions, garlic lemon juice, and white wine vinegar for about 5 minutes over medium heat until tender. Add spinach, and continue to cook over low heat until most of the liquid is gone. Mix in oregano, basil, and ginger; continue cooking for another minute. Add crab meat, slowly mix until cooked through.

3. Scoop crab meat mixture into mushroom tops. Place on lightly greased baking pan and bake for about 15 minutes or until tender.

Tilapia and Veggies Baked in Parchment

This is a super easy one-dish meal.

Servings: 4

Ingredients

- 1 bunch asparagus, washed and trimmed
- 8 small carrots, peeled julienned
- 4 4-ounce tilapia fillets (could substitute cod, halibut, or other whitefish)
- 1 tablespoon olive oil
- 2 cloves garlic, minced
- Juice of 1 lemon
- 1 orange, sliced thin
- Salt and freshly ground black pepper, to taste

Directions

1. Preheat oven to 400 degrees. Cut four 12-inch squares of parchment paper, fold in half.

2. In each packet place 1/4 of asparagus, 1/4 of carrots, 1 piece of tilapia, and 1/4 of garlic. Drizzle with olive oil, squeeze on lemon juice, and sprinkle with salt and pepper. Top with 1-2 orange slices per pouch.

3. Fold parchment paper over fish and vegetables. Fold ends on both sides and arrange pouches on baking sheet.

4. Bake for 12-15 minutes or until fish flakes easily and vegetables are tender.

5. To serve, cut through parchment paper and pull back to expose fish and vegetables.

Wasabi Salmon Burgers

Canned salmon are usually wild salmon that contain one of the highest amounts of omega-3s.

Wasabi provides a distinct Japanese treat.

Servings: 4

Ingredients
- 1/2 teaspoon honey
- 2 tablespoons coconut aminos
- 1 1/2 teaspoons wasabi powder
- 1 egg, lightly beaten
- 12 ounces canned wild salmon, drained
- 2 scallions, finely chopped
- 2 tablespoon fresh ginger, peeled, minced
- 1 teaspoon sesame oil, toasted

Directions

1. In a bowl, combine salmon with egg, ginger, scallions, and oil; mix using a fork to blend well. Form in 4 patties.
2. In a small bowl, whip wasabi powder with coconut aminos and honey, until smooth.
3. In a skillet, heat oil over medium heat and cook patties in batches, for about 4 minutes per side or until firm and browned.
4. Glaze top side with wasabi mixture and cook further for another 15 seconds.

Grilled Shrimp Spiced with Homemade Sriracha

Srirarcha is a spicy chili sauce.

Servings: 2

Ingredients

For the shrimp:

- 1 pound raw shrimp, peeled and deveined
- ¼ cup homemade Sriracha*
- 1 teaspoon garlic powder, divided
- 1 teaspoon chili powder, divided
- 1 teaspoon onion powder, divided
- 1 teaspoon smoked paprika, divided
- ½ teaspoon cumin, divided
- salt and pepper, to taste

For the guacamole:

- 2 avocados, mashed
- ¼ white onion, minced
- 2 garlic cloves, minced

- ¼ teaspoon garlic powder
- ¼ teaspoon cayenne pepper
- juice of ½ a lime
- salt and pepper, to taste

For the Paleo Sriracha:

- 1½ pounds fresh red jalapeño peppers, trimmed, roughly chopped
- 8 garlic cloves, peeled and smashed
- 1/3 cup apple cider vinegar
- 3 tablespoons tomato paste
- 3 tablespoons honey
- 2 tablespoons fish sauce
- 1½ teaspoon kosher salt

Directions

1. Prepare the Sriracha. In a blender, combine all Sriracha ingredients and mix until pureed. Pour into a saucepan and bring to a boil over high heat. Reduce heat to low and simmer for about 10 minutes stirring frequently. Cool and store chilled inside a glass jar with airtight cover.

2. Preheat grill to medium heat.

3. Skew shrimps and place on a chopping board. Brush with Sriracha and sprinkle with spices, salt, and pepper. Do the same with the other side. Grill for about 4 minutes per side or until all pink.

4. Meanwhile prepare the guacamole. Mix all ingredients into a small bowl. Whisk until well blended.

5. Plate individual shrimp skewers with guacamole on the side.

Pan-Seared Salmon on Baby Arugula

Arugula is a rich source of vitamin C and potassium. Salmon is a source of omega-3 fatty acids.

Servings: 2

Ingredients

- 2 (6 oz.) salmon fillets
- 1 1/2 tablespoons olive oil
- 1 1/2 tablespoons fresh lemon juice
- Freshly ground black pepper, to taste

For the salad:

- 3 cups baby arugula leaves
- 2/3 cup grape or cherry tomatoes, halved
- 1/4 cup red onion, thinly slivered
- 1 tablespoon extra-virgin olive oil
- 1 tablespoon red-wine vinegar

Directions

1. In a bowl, marinate salmon with mixture of olive oil, lemon juice, and pepper. Let stand for at least 15 minutes.

2. In a non-stick pan heated over medium-high heat, cook salmon skin side down, for about 3 minutes. Loosen any sticking skin. Lower heat, cover, and continue cooking for about 3 minutes more or until just firm and skin is crispy.

3. Prepare salad by combining the arugula, onion, and tomatoes in a bowl. Add oil and vinegar then season with pepper. Serve at once with the fish.

Baked Fish with Herbed Bacon

Servings: 2

Ingredients
- 1 pound fish (cod, halibut or bass), cut into 2 (8 oz.) pieces
- 1 tablespoon olive oil
- 1 teaspoon lemon juice
- Pinch of cayenne pepper
- salt and pepper, to taste
- 3 tablespoon ghee
- 1 piece of bacon, browned, finely minced
- 2 teaspoon dried parsley
- 1 teaspoon dried basil
- Pinch of garlic powder
- Pinch of salt

Directions

1. Preheat oven to 375 °F. Line a rimmed roasting sheet with parchment paper.

2. Place fish on prepared sheet. Brush with olive oil, drizzle with lemon juice and sprinkle cayenne pepper. Season it with salt and pepper to taste. Roast for about 15-20 minutes or until easily flaked using a fork.

3. Meanwhile, in a bowl combine bacon bits with ghee, parsley, basil, garlic powder, salt and pepper; mix until well blended. Serve fish with bacon mixture on top.

Baked Halibut in Garlicky Sauce

A super-fast meal in 25 minutes that is packed with the goodness of halibut and spiciness of garlic.

Servings: 4

Ingredients

- 1 (3/4 pounds) halibut fillet (1 1/2 inches thick)
- Sea salt and pepper, to taste
- 3 garlic cloves, pressed
- 1/3 cup mayonnaise, whisked
- 2 tablespoons extra-virgin olive oil
- lemon wedges, garnish

Directions

1. Preheat oven to 450°F. Lightly grease a shallow baking dish.

2. Season fish with salt and pepper and place in the prepared baking dish. Add garlic and drizzle with oil.

3. Spread mayonnaise over the fish. Bake for about 15 minutes or until firm and well cooked.

Seared Scallops with Herb-Butter Sauce

These scallops cook up in just a few minutes for a quick yet elegant dinner. Serve with steamed vegetables.

Servings: 2-3

Ingredients
- 1 pound sea scallops
- 1 tablespoon ghee
- 1 tablespoon extra-virgin olive oil
- Sea salt and freshly ground black pepper, to taste
- *For the Herb-Butter Sauce*
- 3 tablespoons ghee
- 1 medium shallot, finely diced
- 1/3 cup apple cider vinegar
- ¼ cup flat-leaf parsley, finely chopped
- ¼ teaspoon lemon zest
- Sea salt and black pepper, to taste
- 2 lemon slices, for serving

Directions

1. Rinse scallops under cold water and pat dry.

2. Heat a nonstick skillet over medium-high heat. Add ghee and olive oil. When oil hot, add scallops in single layer. Season with salt and pepper. Cook 3-4 minutes until one side is crisp and browned. Turn scallops over and sear on other side until crisp and scallops are firm, about 3-4 minutes. Remove scallops from pan and set aside while sauce is prepared.

3. In same pan, add 1 tablespoon of ghee and shallots. Sauté until 2-3 minutes. Add apple cider vinegar and simmer for another 1-2 minutes. Reduce heat to low and add remaining ghee, herbs, and lemon zest. Stir constantly with spoon until ghee is melted.

4. Return scallops to pan and mix gently so sauce is coating them. Add salt and pepper. Serve with lemon slices.

Smoked Salmon Stuffed and Bacon Wrapped Sweet Peppers

These tasty appetizers can be prepared in under 30 minutes.

Servings: 4

Ingredients

- 5 strips of bacon, cut in half
- 10 sweet peppers, halved lengthwise, seeded
- 4 ounces of smoked salmon
- pinch of salt
- Sprinkle of smoked paprika

Directions

1. Preheat oven to 350 °F. Line baking sheet with parchment paper.

2. Stuff peppers with salmon pieces. Sprinkle with some salt and paprika. Wrap bacon around the peppers, securing ends with a toothpick.

3. Place stuffed and wrapped peppers on prepared baking sheet and bake for about 18 minutes or until bacon is browned and crisp.

Sautéed Goan Clams

Servings: 4

Ingredients

- 2 1/4 pounds clams
- 3 tablespoon olive oil
- 4 cloves garlic, chopped
- 1 1/2 inch piece fresh ginger, chopped
- 1 medium onion, chopped
- 2 fresh hot green chili peppers, seeded and chopped
- 2 teaspoon turmeric
- 2 tablespoon ground coriander
- 1 teaspoon cayenne pepper
- 1 cup freshly grated coconut
- 1 tablespoon lemon juice
- 1 tablespoon fresh cilantro, chopped

Directions

1. In a large pot, heat oil over medium-high heat; cook garlic, ginger, onion, and chili peppers for about 4 minutes or until onion turns golden brown. Mix in the ground coriander, turmeric, and cayenne pepper. Add the clams, stir, and cover. Simmer for about 5 minutes. Remove any unopened clams.

2. Serve in bowls, drizzled with lemon juice, and sprinkled with coconut and cilantro.

Vegetables, Fruits, and Salads

Many people think the Paleo diet is all about meat. But nothing could be further from the truth. Vegetables and fruits are a big part of the Paleo way of eating.

Sweet Potato and Leek Hash

This can be served for breakfast or dinner.

Servings: 2

Ingredients

- 3 tablespoon coconut oil, divided
- 2 medium sweet potatoes, peeled, diced
- Sea salt
- ½ teaspoon ground cumin
- ½ teaspoon smoked paprika
- 1 medium leek, diced
- 2 garlic cloves, minced
- 4 whole eggs
- Black pepper to taste

Directions

1. In a large pan, heat 2 tablespoons coconut oil over medium-high heat. Add the sweet potatoes, paprika, cumin, and salt to taste. Mix, cover, and cook for about 5 minutes with occasional stirring until potatoes are nicely browned and crisp. Mix in garlic and leeks; cover and cook for another 5 minutes with occasional stirring or until leeks are tender.

2. Meanwhile, heat remaining tablespoon oil in another pan over medium heat; cook eggs sunny side up. Equally divide sweet potatoes in four plates and top with fried eggs. Sprinkle salt and pepper to taste.

Zoodles

A vegetable spiral slicer is one of the most useful tools in the Paleo kitchen and will make preparing zucchini noodles a snap. Serve these Zoodles with meatballs for a delicious Paleo meal. These can also be made by hand using a julienne peeler.

Servings: 4

Ingredients

- 4 medium zucchini
- Salt and freshly ground pepper to taste

Directions

1. Using either your vegetable spiral slicer or julienne peeler, cut zucchini into long skinny noodles.

2. These can be cooked by stir frying in either olive oil or coconut oil for 2-3 minutes until tender or can be microwaved in a covered, microwave-safe dish for about 1.5 to 2 minutes.

Stir-Fried Vegetables with Toasted Cumin Seeds

This veggie stir-fry cooks up quick for a meatless dinner option. Serve with Cauli-rice.

Servings: 6

Ingredients

- 1 teaspoon ground cumin seeds, toasted
- 2 tablespoons coconut oil
- 1/2 teaspoon freshly cracked black peppercorns
- 1/2 teaspoon cumin seeds
- 3/4 teaspoon ground coriander
- 1/2 jalapeño, finely chopped
- 6 cups green cabbage, thinly sliced
- 2 cups carrots, grated
- 1/2 cup loosely packed fresh cilantro sprigs, finely chopped
- 3 tablespoon fresh lime juice

Directions

1. In a large saucepan, heat oil over medium-high heat and cook peppercorns, coriander, and remaining 1/2 teaspoon cumin seeds for about 2 minutes or until browned. Mix in jalapeño, and cooked for another 45 seconds until just tender. Add carrots and cabbage cook and stir for about 4 minutes or until cabbage starts to softened.

2. Stir in cumin and cook for about 30 seconds. Put off heat and stir in lime juice and cilantro. Add more seasonings to taste.

Zucchini Pancake Fritters

Zucchini is one of the most versatile vegetables. Make these pancakes when you have an abundance of zucchini in the garden for a delicious treat.

Servings: 4

Ingredients

- 2 medium zucchini, finely grated
- 1 medium Vivaldi onion, finely chopped
- ½ cup almond flour
- 2 eggs, lightly beaten
- ¼ cup coconut milk
- Juice of ½ lemon
- Salt and freshly ground black pepper, to taste
- 2 tablespoons coconut oil for frying

Directions

1. In a bowl, mix zucchini, onion, flour, eggs, coconut milk, lemon juice, salt, and pepper.

2. Heat coconut oil in non-stick skillet over medium-high heat for several minutes until hot.

3. Add zucchini mixture to hot pan in ¼ cup portions. Cook on one side until light golden brown, about 2-3 minutes. Flip with spatula, and cook on other side until light golden brown, another 2-3 minutes. Remove from pan and place on paper-towel lined plate.

4. Serve with apple sauce.

Sweet Potato and Coconut Curry

This is a mild curry that makes a delicious side to fish or chicken.

Servings: 4

Ingredients

- 1 tablespoon coconut oil
- 1 small yellow onion, diced
- 3 clove garlic, minced
- 1 teaspoon cumin powder
- ½ teaspoon turmeric
- ½ teaspoon cardamom
- ½ teaspoon cinnamon
- ½ teaspoon ground ginger
- 1 can diced tomatoes
- 2 medium sweet potatoes, peeled and cut into bit-size cubes
- 1 can (15 ounces) coconut milk
- Salt and freshly ground black pepper, to taste
- Flat leaf parsley for garnish

Directions

1. Heat coconut oil in a deep skillet over medium-high heat. Add onion and sauté for 2-3 minutes until onion starts to soften. Add garlic and spices and sauté for another 1-2 minutes.

2. Add tomatoes, sweet potatoes, and coconut milk to pan. Season with salt and pepper. Turn heat down to low, cover pan, and let simmer for about 30 minutes or until sweet potatoes are tender. Taste and add more spices if desired.

3. Serve hot, topped with fresh parsley for garnish.

Cauliflower "Rice"

Cauliflower "Rice" or Cauli-Rice can be made ahead in large batches and then frozen, making it super convenient for quick weeknight dinners.

Servings: 6

Ingredients

- 1 large head of cauliflower
- Food processor or hand grater

Directions

1. Wash cauliflower and remove leaves. Cut cauliflower florets off of core; discard core.

2. Place florets into food processor (will need to be done in batches). Pulse until cauliflower is reduced to rice-sized pieces. Alternatively, use hand grater to grate cauliflower.

3. Cauliflower rice can now either be frozen for later use or cooked in a variety of ways depending on the dish.

- **Bake:** Spread cauliflower rice on baking sheet lined with parchment paper and bake in 400 degree oven for about 15 minutes, turning once halfway through.

- **Fry:** Heat olive oil or coconut oil in skillet over medium-high heat. Add cauliflower rice and sauté for 4-5 minutes. Season with salt and pepper.

- **Microwave:** Place cauliflower rice in microwave safe dish. Cover and cook in microwave for 1-2 minutes, until tender.

Cauliflower Mashed "Potatoes"

This recipes used almond milk and ghee for very authentic tasting mashed "potatoes."

Servings: 4

Ingredients

- 1 large head cauliflower
- ¼ cup almond milk (use a little more or less depending on desired consistency)
- 1-2 tablespoons ghee
- Salt and freshly ground black pepper, to taste

Directions

1. Wash cauliflower and remove leaves. Cut cauliflower florets off of core; discard core.

2. Fill large pot with 2-3 inches of water and heat over medium-high heat. Add cauliflower florets to pot and cover. Cook until cauliflower is very soft, about 10 minutes. Turn off heat, drain water from pot, keeping cauliflower in pot.

3. Add milk, ghee, salt, and pepper to pot with cauliflower. Use a potato masher or immersion blender to mash cauliflower to desired consistency. Serve hot.

Roasted Balsamic Vegetables

Feel free to substitute whatever vegetables you have on hand for this recipe.

Servings: 4

Ingredients

- 2 cups butternut squash, cubed
- 1½ cup broccoli florets, chopped
- ½ red onion, chopped
- 1 zucchini, chopped
- ½ red bell pepper, chopped
- 1 large garlic clove, minced
- 2 tablespoon olive oil
- 1 tablespoon balsamic vinegar
- 1½ teaspoon fresh rosemary
- ½ teaspoon sea salt
- ½ teaspoon black pepper

Directions

1. Preheat oven to 425 °F.

2. In a bowl, combine oil, rosemary, vinegar, salt, and pepper; mix to blend. Mix in the vegetables, stir to coat thoroughly. Evenly spread on a parchment-lined baking sheet and roast for about 40 minutes or until squash is just softened.

Coconut Lime Fruit Salad

Servings: 4

Ingredients

- 2 cups strawberries, halved
- 2 cups honeydew melon, chopped into cubes
- 1 mango, chopped
- 1/4 cup coconut milk
- 4 teaspoon fresh lime juice
- 2 teaspoon fresh basil, chopped
- 1/2 teaspoon raw honey
- Dash of sea salt

Directions

1. In a salad bowl, combine the fruits. In another bowl, whisk coconut milk with lime juice, honey and basil. Season with some salt. Pour dressing onto fruit. Toss to blend. Enjoy.

Tangy Roasted Broccoli with Garlic

Servings: 6

Ingredients

- 2 heads broccoli, cut into florets
- 1 clove garlic, minced
- 2 teaspoon extra-virgin olive oil
- 1 teaspoon sea salt
- 1/2 teaspoon ground black pepper
- 1/2 teaspoon lemon juice

Directions

1. Preheat oven to 400 °F.

2. In a bowl, combine oil, garlic salt, and black pepper. Add broccoli. Toss to coat. Evenly scatter broccoli on a baking sheet and roast for about 18 minutes or until fork tender.

3. Plate and drizzle with lemon juice. Serve at once.

Fried Brussels Sprouts

Servings: 4

Ingredients

- 1 pound Brussels sprout, whole
- 5 tablespoon coconut oil
- 4 garlic cloves, minced
- Dash of lemon juice, for garnish
- Sea salt, to taste
- Black pepper, to taste

Directions

1. In a pan, heat oil over medium heat. Add whole Brussel sprouts, stir and cook for about 5 minutes or until browned but not charred.

2. Mix in garlic and cook for another minute or until garlic turns light brown. Sprinkle salt and pepper to taste. Drizzle lemon juice. Serve warm.

3. *Optional:* Add some shredded coconut along with garlic for a different flavor.

Asparagus Wrapped in Bacon

These make fancy-looking side dishes and are very easy to prepare.

Servings: 4

Ingredients

- 1 bunch asparagus (about 1 ½ pounds), ends trimmed
- 2 tablespoons extra-virgin olive oil
- Salt and freshly ground black pepper, to taste
- 4 slices bacon
- Lemon wedges for serving.

Directions

1. Drizzle olive oil over asparagus spears to lightly coat. Season with salt and pepper.

2. Divide asparagus spears into 4 bundles. Wrap a slice of bacon securely around each bundle.

3. Arrange asparagus bundles on slotted broiler pan. Bake in preheated 450 degree oven 15-18 minutes, turning once, until bacon is crisp and asparagus is tender. Serve with lemon wedges.

Collard Greens with Bacon

Servings: 4

Ingredients

- 4 slices bacon, cut into small pieces
- 1 medium onion, chopped
- 4 garlic cloves, minced
- 6 cups collard greens, tough stems removed and cleaned well
- 1 teaspoon sea salt
- 1 teaspoon black pepper
- 1 1/2 cups low-sodium chicken stock

Directions

1. In a large sauce pan, cook bacon until browned. Mix in garlic and onions and cook for about 3 minutes or until tender and browned.

2. Add collard greens and broth, mix to blend, cover and cook over medium heat for about 30 minutes or until tender.

3. Season with salt and pepper and serve warm.

Carrots with Tart Cherries

Carrots are honey glazed with tart cherries, considered to contain some of the highest anti-inflammatory properties among all foods.

Servings: 4

Ingredients

- 5 carrots, sliced
- 2 tablespoons butter
- 1 1/2 tablespoon honey
- 1/4 cup dried cherries

Directions

1. Cook carrots in a saucepan with enough boiling water to cover for about 10 minutes or until tender. Remove liquid and set aside in a bowl.

2. In the same saucepan, heat butter over medium heat until melted; mix in honey until smooth. Add in cherries, simmer over low heat for about a minute. Turn off heat, add in cooked carrots and gently mix to coat.

Soups and Stews

Spiced Ginger Carrot Soup

Servings: 6

Ingredients

- 3 tablespoons olive oil
- 1/2 teaspoon yellow mustard seeds, ground
- 1 teaspoon coriander seeds, ground
- 1/2 teaspoon curry powder
- 1 tbsp. fresh ginger, peeled, minced
- 1 1/2 lbs. carrots, peeled, thinly sliced
- 2 cups onions, chopped
- 1 1/2 teaspoon lime zest, finely grated
- 5 cups low-salt vegetable broth
- 2 teaspoon fresh lime juice
- Black pepper, to taste

Directions

1. In a heavy saucepan, heat olive oil over medium-high heat. Stir and cook ground seeds and curry powder for about a minute. Mix in ginger and cook for another minute. Stir in carrots, onions, and lime zest. Stir and cook for another 3 minutes until onions are tender.

2. Pour in broth and bring to a low boil. Lower heat and simmer for about 30 minutes or until carrots are softened. Set aside to slightly cool.

3. Puree the mixture using a food processor—you may need to work in batches.

4. Return puree to saucepan. Adjust to desired consistency by adding more broth as needed. Mix in lime juice then add black pepper to taste. Serve hot.

Asian Shrimp and Coconut Soup

Servings: 6-8

Ingredients

- 1 tablespoon coconut oil
- 3 garlic cloves, minced
- 1 tablespoon freshly grated ginger
- 5 cups chicken broth
- 1 cup snow peas, cut in half
- 1 cup matchstick carrots
- 1/2 cup coconut milk
- 1 pound medium shrimp, precooked, tails removed

Directions

1. Heat coconut oil in large saucepan on medium heat. Add garlic and ginger and cook for 1 minute. Pour in chicken broth, turn heat to high, and bring to low boil.

2. Add in snow peas and carrots, reduce heat to medium and cook for 3-4 minutes.

3. Stir in coconut milk and shrimp. Continue cooking for another 3-4 minutes or until shrimp are heated through.

Easy Chicken, Kale, and Carrot Soup

This healthy soup is quick to prepare and satisfying to eat.

Servings: 6-8

Ingredients

- 1 tablespoon olive oil
- 1 medium yellow onion, diced
- 2 cloves garlic, minced
- 5-6 large carrots, sliced thin
- 2 boneless, skinless chicken breasts, cut into small pieces
- 4 cups chicken broth, store bought or homemade
- 1 head of kale, chopped
- Salt and freshly ground pepper to taste

Directions

1. Heat olive oil in large pot over medium heat. Add onion and garlic and saute for 2-3 minutes until onions start to soften.

2. Add carrot, chicken, and chicken broth to pot. Simmer for 35-40 minutes, or until chicken is fully cooked. Add kale to pot and simmer for an additional 5 minutes. Season with salt and pepper to taste.

Cream of Broccoli Soup

Cauliflower and almond milk give this soup its creamy texture.

Servings: 4

Ingredients

- 1 tablespoon extra-virgin olive oil
- 1 medium yellow onion, chopped
- 3 garlic cloves, minced
- 1 small head cauliflower, chopped into florets
- 2 cups almond milk, unsweetened
- 2 cups chicken broth
- 3 cups broccoli florets, chopped
- Salt and freshly ground black pepper, to taste

Directions

1. Heat olive oil in large saucepan over medium-high heat. Add onions and garlic and sauté for 2-3 minutes until onion turns translucent.

2. Add cauliflower, almond milk, chicken broth, and broccoli. Cover pot and bring to boil. Reduce heat and simmer, covered, for 10 minutes or until cauliflower and broccoli florets are soft.

3. Pour mixture into blender or food processor and puree until smooth (may need to be done in two batches). Return to pot. Season with salt and pepper and simmer on low for an additional 10 minutes. Serve hot.

Chicken, Zucchini, and Carrot Soup

Servings: 6

Ingredients

- 6 cups chicken broth
- 1 whole chicken, quartered
- 1 yellow onion, diced
- 2 cloves garlic, minced
- 1 teaspoon black pepper
- 1 bay leaf
- 6 fresh tomatoes, diced
- 2 small zucchini, thinly sliced
- 3 carrots, diced

Directions

1. In a pot, combine broth, chicken, garlic, onion, black pepper, and bay leaf; bring to a boil over high heat. Lower heat and simmer for about 15-20 minutes or until chicken is well cooked. Remove chicken into a bowl using slotted spoon, allow to cool. Remove meat from chicken, chop meat, and return it to the pot. Discard bones and the bay leaf.

2. Add in tomatoes, zucchini, and carrots and cook on low heat for another 20 minutes or until vegetables are tender. Divide into soup bowls and serve.

Zucchini and Leek with Roasted Garlic Soup

Servings: 6

Ingredients

- 2½ pounds zucchini, cubed
- 1 leek, chopped
- ½ yellow onion, chopped
- 3 cloves of garlic, peeled
- 2 tablespoons coconut oil, melted
- ½ cup raw cashews
- 2½ cups filtered water
- Salt and pepper to taste

Directions

1. Preheat oven to 400 °F.

2. Spread zucchini, leek, onion, and garlic on a paper-lined cookie sheet. Drizzle with coconut oil and roast for about 20 minutes or until zucchini is fork tender.

3. Put roasted veggies into a food processor, add in cashews and water. Process until smooth and creamy.

4. Transfer puree into a large pot and heat to near boiling over high heat. Lower heat and simmer for about 5 minutes. Season with salt and pepper. Serve hot.

Paleo Avgolemono

Avgolemono is Greek chicken lemon soup. This Paleo version replaces the traditional rice with cauliflower rice.

Servings: 6

Ingredients
- 3 tablespoons ghee
- 1 large yellow onion, diced
- 3 stalks celery, diced
- ¼ cup arrowroot flour
- 8 cups chicken stock
- Salt and freshly ground black pepper, to taste
- Juice from 2-3 lemons
- 3 cups Cauliflower Rice
- 2 cups cooked chicken
- 6 eggs yolks, beaten

Directions

1. Heat ghee in large pot over medium heat. Add onion and celery and saute for 2-3 minutes, until onion becomes translucent.

2. Add in arrowroot flour and cook, stirring, for 1 minute. Add chicken stock, lemon juice, salt, and pepper. Stir well.

3. Add Cauliflower Rice and bring to boil. Reduce heat to medium-low and simmer, covered for 15 minutes.

4. Add in chicken. Taste and season with additional salt, pepper, and lemon, as desired.

5. To bowl with beaten egg yolks, slowly add ½ cup of soup mixture, stirring constantly. Add egg and soup mixture to pot. Simmer for an addition 5-10 minutes, being careful not to let soup boil.

6. Serve hot. Garnish with lemon slices.

Pumpkin and Bacon Soup

Servings: 2

Ingredients

- 4 slices bacon
- 1/2 large pumpkin, peeled, seeded, cubed
- 1 large white onion, finely chopped
- 2 cloves garlic, minced
- 1 tablespoon fresh thyme
- 2 cups chicken broth

Directions

1. In a pan, brown bacon over medium high heat. Transfer onto a chopping board, reserving the generated grease. Chop bacon to 1-inch pieces.

2. Into the same pan with bacon grease, add the onion and garlic; fry for about 5 minutes over low heat.

3. Add the pumpkin cubes along with the stock. Bring to a boil and let simmer for about 25 minutes.

4. Transfer mixture into a blender and puree until smooth. Pour back into the pot, mix in thyme and bacon. Serve immediately.

Sauces, Dips, and Condiments

Guacamole

Servings: 4

Ingredients

- 2 avocados, mashed
- ¼ white onion, minced
- 2 garlic cloves, minced
- ¼ teaspoon garlic powder
- ¼ teaspoon cayenne pepper
- juice of ½ a lime
- salt and pepper, to taste

Directions

1. Mix all ingredients into a small bowl. Whisk until well blended.

Fresh Tomato Salsa

Make up a big batch to keep on hand. Flavors get better as they meld together.

Servings: Makes 2 ½ cups

Ingredients

- 2 pounds roma tomatoes, diced
- 2 serrano or jalapeno chilies, deseeded and finely chopped
- 1/3 white onion, finely chopped
- ½ cup fresh cilantro
- 1 garlic clove, minced
- 1 ½ tablespoons lime juice
- Salt and freshly ground black pepper, to taste

Directions

1. Mix together all ingredients in a bowl. Taste and more lime juice, salt, and pepper, as desired. Serve at once or refrigerate for up to a week.

Basil Pesto

This recipe omits the traditional Parmesan cheese. If you include cheese in your diet, feel free to add it in.

Servings: Makes about 1 cup

Ingredients

- 2 cups fresh basil leaves
- ½ cup pine nuts
- 2 garlic cloves, finely minced
- Salt and black pepper, to taste
- ½ cup extra-virgin olive oil

Directions

1. Add basil, nuts, garlic, salt, and pepper to food processor. Pulse until finely chopped.
2. Add in olive oil and puree until smooth.

Paleo Mayonnaise

Store bought mayonnaise is full of soybean oil and fillers. Making your own Paleo mayonnaise is easy and much healthier.

Servings: Makes 1 ¼ cups

Ingredients

- 2 egg yolks
- 1 teaspoon mustard powder
- 1 teaspoon white vinegar
- 2 teaspoons lemon juice
- 1 cup olive oil

Directions

1. Make sure all ingredients are at room temperature (this is important, mayo won't properly emulsify if ingredients are cold).

2. In a bowl, whisk together egg yolks, mustard powder, vinegar, and lemon juice. Slowly add in olive oil, ¼ cup at a time, whisking continuously until mixture has thickened.

3. Store in refrigerator.

Marinara Sauce

This marinara sauce only takes about half an hour to prepare and easily beats out any jarred version.

Servings: 6 cups

Ingredients

- ¼ cup extra-virgin olive oil
- ½ small yellow onion, diced
- 4 cloves garlic, minced
- 3 (28-ounce) cans whole, peeled tomatoes, chopped
- 1 teaspoon thyme
- 2 teaspoons oregano
- ¼ cup fresh basil, finely chopped
- 2 teaspoons sea salt
- Freshly ground black pepper, to taste

Directions

1. In a saucepan, heat olive oil over medium-high heat. Add onion and garlic and sauté for 3-4 minutes. Add tomatoes and herbs. Bring to boil and then reduce heat to low. Simmer for about 20-25 minutes. Season with salt and pepper.

Honey Mustard Sauce

Use this as a marinade or a dipping sauce for chicken fingers.

Servings: About 1 cup of sauce

Ingredients

- 1/2 cup extra-virgin olive oil
- ¼ cup apple cider vinegar
- 2 tablespoons brown mustard
- 2 tablespoons Dijon mustard
- 3 tablespoons honey (use more or less depending on desired sweetness)
- 1 teaspoon sea salt
- 1 teaspoon freshly ground black pepper

Directions

1. Whisk all ingredients together in a bowl. Store in glass container in refrigerator.

Desserts, Treats, and Snacks

Who says you can't indulge your sweet tooth on the Paleo diet?

Coconut Date Bites

Dates are naturally sweet.

Servings: 4

Ingredients

- 20 dates, pitted
- 1 tablespoon almond butter
- 1/3 cup coconut flakes, desiccated

Directions

1. Into the bowl of a blender, combine dates with almond butter; blend until smooth. Form batter into golf-size balls. A little oil on the hands will help ease the work.

2. Roll the balls on coconut flakes and freeze for at least 20 minutes.

Curried Zucchini Chips

Servings: 4

Ingredients

- 2 medium zucchinis, thinly sliced
- 1 tablespoon olive oil
- ¼ teaspoon curry powder
- ⅛ teaspoon garlic powder
- ⅛ teaspoon salt

Directions

1. Preheat oven to 325 °F. Lightly grease 2 paper-lined baking sheets.

2. Arrange zucchini slices in single layer on the prepared baking sheets. Drizzle olive oil and sprinkle with curry powder, garlic powder, and salt.

3. Bake for about an hour or until very crisp. Cool and store in an airtight container

Kale Chips

Next time you are craving potato chips, reach for these low-cal snacks instead.

Servings: 6

Ingredients

- 1 large bunch kale
- 2 tablespoons olive oil
- 1 ½ teaspoons sea salt

Directions

1. Preheat oven to 350 degrees. Line cookie sheet with parchment paper.

2. Cut stems from kale. Wash and thoroughly dry kale leaves.

3. Spread kale out on baking sheet in single layer. Drizzle with olive oil and season with salt.

4. Bake until edges are browned, about 10-12 minutes.

Lemon Almond Meal Cake & Blueberry Cream

Servings: 6

Ingredients

For cake
- 1 cup almond meal
- 1/2 cup tapioca flour
- 2/3 teaspoon gluten free baking powder
- 3 eggs, at room temperature
- 4 tablespoon melted ghee
- Zest from 1 lemon
- Juice from 1 lemon
- 4 tablespoons maple syrup

For topping
- 1 cup coconut cream, chilled
- 2 tablespoons fresh blueberries
- 1 tablespoon lemon juice
- 1 tablespoon honey
- A few fresh blueberries and lemon zest as garnish

Directions

1. Preheat oven to 375 °F. Lightly grease a paper-lined baking pan.

2. In a bowl, whisk eggs with maple syrup using hand mixer for about 4 minutes or until smooth and its volume is doubled. Add almond meal and tapioca, then melted ghee, lemon juice, and zest. Mix some more until fully blended.

3. Spread batter into prepared pan and bake for 20 minutes. Cool on wire rack, then remove from pan and peel off parchment paper. Allow to cool.

4. Meanwhile prepare the topping. Puree the berries into a food processor. Add some water if needed. Into a bowl, add coconut cream. Add pureed berries and mix.

5. Brush cake with honey and drizzle with lemon juice. Liberally glaze cake with berry-coconut cream mixture. Garnish with fresh berries and extra lemon zest.

Paleo Honey Cake

Servings: 8

Ingredients

- 2 1/2 cups blanched almond flour
- 1/2 teaspoon sea salt
- 1 teaspoon baking soda
- 1 tablespoon cinnamon
- 1/2 cup honey
- 1/4 teaspoon cloves
- 1/2 cup coconut oil
- 4 eggs
- 1/2 cup raisins

Directions

1. Preheat oven to 350 °F. Lightly grease and flour 8-inch cake pan.

2. Into a large bowl, combine almond flour, cinnamon, salt, baking soda, and cloves. Mix well to blend.

3. In a separate bowl, whip eggs. Mix in honey, and coconut oil until smooth. Slowly mix the wet ingredients into the dry ingredients until batter is formed. Fold in raisins.

4. Transfer the batter to the cake pan and bake for about 33 minutes or until toothpick comes out clean when inserted. Cool on wire rack.

Coconut Chocolate Truffles

The hands on time for these truffles is short, but they do require some time in the freezer to set, so plan accordingly.

Servings: About 12 truffles

Ingredients

- 4 ounces dark chocolate (70%)
- 1 tablespoon coconut oil
- ¼ cup coconut milk, room temperature
- 1 teaspoon honey
- Unsweetened shredded coconut, for rolling

Directions

1. Break chocolate into pieces and place in a microwave safe dish. Microwave chocolate until melted, checking every 30 seconds (about 1 ½ to 2 minutes depending on microwave).

2. In a separate bowl, melt the coconut oil. Add to chocolate mixture. Pour in coconut milk and honey. Stir well to combine.

3. Place in freezer for 2 hours. Remove from freezer and scoop out teaspoon-size chunks. Form into balls using hands. Roll balls in shredded coconut.

Fudgy Chocolate Brownies

The fudgy brownies are perfect when you need a chocolate fix.

Servings: 12

Ingredients

- 6 tablespoons ghee
- 8 ounces bittersweet chocolate chips
- 2/3 cup coconut sugar
- ½ teaspoon sea salt
- 1 teaspoon vanilla extract
- 2 eggs
- 1/3 cup almond meal flour
- 1 tablespoon coconut flour

Directions

1. Preheat oven to 350 degrees. Lightly grease a 8-inch square pan.

2. Place butter and chocolate chips into a microwave-safe dish. Microwave until butter and chocolate are melted, checking every 30 seconds (should take about 1 ½ to 2 minutes).

3. In a mixing bowl, mix sugar salt, and vanilla extract. Beat in eggs. Stir in melted chocolate mixture. Add in almond flour and coconut flour, stir until well blended.

4. Pour batter into prepared pan. Bake for 25-30 minutes. Test for doneness by inserting toothpick in center. Cool before cutting.

Carrot Chocolate Cookies

Servings: 12

Ingredients

- 1 cup coconut flour
- 1/2 cup tapioca flour
- 2 large carrots (shredded)
- 1 cup coconut sugar
- 1 cup coconut oil, (melted)
- 2 pastured eggs (beaten)
- 1 teaspoon vanilla
- 1/2 teaspoon pumpkin pie spice
- ½ teaspoon sea salt
- ¾ cup unsweetened chocolate chips

Directions

1. Preheat oven to 350 °F. Line a cookie sheet with parchment paper.

2. In a bowl, whisk eggs. Add oil, sugar, and vanilla. Mix to blend. Add carrots, mix until well incorporated. Add flours and spices. Mix well. Fold in chocolate chips.

3. Spoon batter onto prepared baking sheet, press to flatten and bake for about 35 minutes.

Baked Apples with Walnuts, Honey, and Cinnamon

These cinnamon apples are perfect on a cool autumn day.

Servings: Makes 8 servings

Ingredients
- 2 teaspoons cinnamon
- ½ cup honey
- 8 ounces walnuts, coarsely chopped
- 8 large apples
- 1 tablespoon lemon juice

Directions

1. Preheat oven to 375°F.

2. In a mixing bowl, mix together cinnamon, honey, and walnuts.

3. Core apples, scoop out enough of the insides to make room for nut stuffing. Place apples in baking dish.

4. Spoon nut filling into each apple. Drizzle a little lemon juice on top of each apple.

5. Bake in oven for 30-35 minutes or until apples are soft.

Paleo Pumpkin Muffins

Servings: 6

Ingredients

- 1 1/2 cups almond flour
- 1 teaspoon baking powder
- 1 teaspoon baking soda
- 1/2 teaspoon ground cinnamon
- 1 1/2 teaspoon pumpkin pie spice
- 1/8 teaspoon sea salt
- 3/4 cup canned pumpkin
- 3 large eggs
- 1/4 cup raw honey
- 2 teaspoon almond butter

Directions

1. Preheat oven to 350 °F. Lightly grease muffin cups.

2. In a bowl, combine flour with the next 5 ingredients. In a separate bowl, whisk eggs; mix in honey until smooth. Gradually pour mixture into flour mixture, mix until batter is formed.

3. Bake for about 25 minutes on the middle rack of oven, or until golden brown.

From the Author

I hope you enjoyed the *Primal Paleo Cookbook* and that it helps you create easy, healthy Paleo meals for you and your family to enjoy!

Please check out our other titles in the Paleo cooking series:

Paleo Diet: Beginner's Paleo Cooking for Health and Weight Loss

Mediterranean Paleo

Slow Cooker Paleo: Healthy, Quick, and Easy Paleo Recipes for Your Slow Cooker

Asian Paleo

Paleo Autoimmune Protocol: Paleo Recipes and Meal Plan to Heal Your Body

More Bestselling Titles from Dylanna Press

Mason Jar Meals by Dylanna Press

Mason jar meals are a fun and practical way to take your meals on the go. Mason jars are an easy way to prepare individual servings, so whether you're cooking for one, two, or a whole crowd, these fun, make-ahead meals will work.

Includes More than 50 Recipes and Full-Color Photos

In this book, you'll find a wide variety of recipes including all kinds of salads, as well as hot meal ideas such as mini chicken pot pies and lasagna in a jar. Also included are mouth-watering desserts such as strawberry shortcake, apple pie, and s'mores.

The recipes are easy to prepare and don't require any special cooking skills. So what are you waiting for? Grab your Mason jars and start preparing these gorgeous and tasty dishes!

Beat Pain, Slow Aging, and Reduce Risk of Heart Disease with the Inflammation Diet

Inflammation has been called the "silent killer" and it has been linked to a wide variety of illnesses including heart disease, arthritis, diabetes, chronic pain, autoimmune disorders, and cancer.

Often, the root of chronic inflammation is in the foods we eat.

The Inflammation Diet: Complete Guide to Beating Pain and Inflammation will show you how, by making simple changes to your diet, you can greatly reduce inflammation in your body and reduce your symptoms and lower your risk of chronic disease.

The book includes a complete plan for eliminating inflammation and implementing an anti-inflammatory diet:

• Overview of inflammation and the body's immune response – what can trigger it and why chronic inflammation is harmful
• The link between diet and inflammation
• Inflammatory foods to avoid
• Anti-inflammatory foods to add to your diet to beat pain and inflammation
• Over 50 delicious inflammation diet recipes
• A 14-day meal plan

Take charge of your health and implement the inflammation diet to lose weight, slow the aging process, eliminate chronic pain, and reduce the likelihood and symptoms of chronic disease.

Learn how to heal your body from within through diet.

Index

A
almonds
    Coconut Fruit and Nut Granola, 29
    Lemon Almond Meal Cake with Blueberry Cream, 160
apples
    Baked Apples with Walnuts, Honey and Cinnamon, 166
    Banana Apple Smoothie with Greens, 30
    Cran-Apple Chicken Salad, 38
Apricot-Mango Salsa, 76
Asian Chicken Lettuce Wraps, 46
Asian Shrimp and Coconut Soup, 136
Asian-Style Short Ribs, 70
Asparagus Wrapped in Bacon, 128
Avgolemono, Paleo, 143
avocado
    Grilled Chicken Salad with Mango and Avocado, 44
    Guacamole, 146
    Shrimp and Avocado Ceviche, 92

B
bacon
    Asparagus Wrapped in Bacon, 128
    Bacon and Egg Omelet Muffins, 24
    Baked Eggs with Tomato and Bacon, 22
    Baked Fish with Herbed Bacon, 16
    Collard Greens with Bacon, 130
    Pumpkin and Bacon Soup, 144
    Smoked Salmon Stuffed and Bacon Wrapped Sweet Peppers, 110
Banana Apple Smoothie with Greens, 30
Basil Pesto, 149
beef
    Asian-Style Short Ribs, 70
    Beef and Broccoli Fried Cauli-Rice, 72–73
    Beef and Veggie Kebabs with Spicy Mediterranean Marinade, 66–67
    Beef and Veggie Stir Fry wth Ginger-Orange Sauce, 60
    Beef Stew with Butternut Squash, 62
    Grilled Steak with Ginger Marinade, 69
    Paleo Chili, 56
    Portobello Burger, 58
    Roasted Pepper Stuffed with Spinach, Walnuts, and Ground Beef, 64
    Slow Cooker Beef Ragu with Zoodles, 59
    Slow Cooker Short Ribs, 68
    Yummy Homestyle Meatloaf, 63
bell pepper, *see* peppers
broccoli
    Beef and Broccoli Fried Cauli-Rice, 72–73
    Beef and Veggie Stir Fry wth Ginger-Orange Sauce, 60
    Cream of Broccoli Soup, 138
    Roasted Balsamic Vegetables, 124
    Tangy Roasted Broccoli with Garlic, 126
    Teriyaki Chicken Stir-Fry, 48
Brownies, Fudgy Chocolate, 164
Brussels Sprouts, Fried, 127
burgers
    Bun-Less Paleo Turkey Burgers, 44
    Portobello Burger, 58
    Wasabi Salmon Burgers, 100

C
cabbage:Stir-Fried Vegetables with Toasted Cumin Seeds, 117
cakes
    Lemon Almond Meal Cake with Blueberry Cream, 160
    Paleo Honey Cake, 161
carrots
    Carrot Chocolate Cookies, 165

Carrots with Tart Cherries, 131
Chicken, Zucchini, and Carrot Soup, 140
Easy Chicken, Kale, and Carrot Soup, 137
Spiced Ginger Carrot Soup, 134
Stir-Fried Vegetables with Toasted Cumin Seeds, 117

cauliflower
Beef and Broccoli Fried Cauli-Rice, 72–73
Cauliflower Mashed "Potatoes," 123
Cauliflower "Rice," 122

chicken
Asian Chicken Lettuce Wraps, 46
Chicken, Zucchini, and Carrot Soup, 140
Chicken Piccata, 42
Cran-Apple Chicken Salad, 38
Crispy Coconut Chicken Fingers with Honey Mustard Sauce, 40
Crunchy-Spicy Baked Chicken Drumsticks, 39
Curried Chicken Stew, 41
Easy Chicken, Kale, and Carrot Soup, 137
Grilled Chicken Salad with Mango and Avocado, 44
Honey Orange Chicken, 48
Paleo Chicken and Mushrooms, 50
Paleo Teriyaki Wings, 37
Teriyaki Chicken Stir-Fry, 49

chili
Paleo Chili, 56
Turkey Pumpkin Chili, 53

chocolate
Carrot Chocolate Cookies, 165
Coconut Chocolate Truffles, 163
Fudgy Chocolate Brownies, 164

Citrus Baked Salmon, 88
Clams, Sautéed Goan, 111

coconut
Asian Shrimp and Coconut Soup, 136
Coconut Chocolate Truffles, 163
Coconut Date Bites, 156
Coconut Flour Pancakes, 23
Coconut Fruit and Nut Granola, 29
Coconut Lime Fruit Salad, 125
Crispy Coconut Chicken Fingers with Honey Mustard Sauce, 40
Sweet Potato and Coconut Curry, 120

Cod, Mediterranean, 91
Collard Greens with Bacon, 130

Cookies, Carrot Chocolate, 165
Crab and Spinach-Stuffed Mushrooms, 97
Cran-Apple Chicken Salad, 38

curries
Curried Chicken Stew, 41
Curried Zucchini Chips, 157
Sweet Potato and Coconut Curry, 120

D
Date Bites, Coconut, 156

dips
Fresh Tomato Salsa, 148
Guacamole, 146

E
Easy Paleo Breakfast Scramble, 20

eggs
Bacon and Egg Omelet Muffins, 24
Baked Eggs with Tomato and Bacon, 22
Easy Paleo Breakfast Scramble, 20
Egg Salad, 28
Paleo Vegetable Omelet, 16
Zucchini, Red Pepper, and Sweet Potato Frittata, 18
Zucchini and Red Pepper Shakshuka, 33

F
fish
Baked Fish with Herbed Bacon, 16
Baked Halibut in Garlicky Sauce, 107
Citrus Baked Salmon, 88
Healthy, Yummy Real Tuna Salad, 96
Italian-Style Tuna Stuffed Peppers, 86
Mediterranean Cod, 91
Pan-Seared Salmon on Baby Arugula, 105
Pecan-Crusted Fish with Oranga Salsa, 89
Smoked Salmon Stuffed and Bacon Wrapped Sweet Peppers, 110
Tilapia and Veggies Baked in Parchment, 99
Wasabi Salmon Burgers, 100

freezer items, 6

frittata
Zucchini, Red Pepper, and Sweet Potato Frittata, 18

Fudgy Chocolate Brownies, 164

G
Ginger-Orange Sauce, 60
Granola, Coconut Fruit and Nut, 29
Greek-Style Lamb Meatballs, 80
Guacamole, 146

H
Halibut in Garlicky Sauce, Baked, 107
Honey Cake, Paleo, 161
Honey Mustard Sauce, 40, 153
Honey Orange Chicken, 48

I
Italian-Style Tuna Stuffed Peppers, 86

K
kale
    Easy Chicken, Kale, and Carrot Soup, 137
    Kale Chips, 158
    Spanish Chorizo Stew with Sweet Potatoes and Kale, 75
kitchen, stocking your, 5–7

L
lamb
    Easy, Tasty Lamb Chops, 82
    Greek-Style Lamb Meatballs, 80
leeks
    Sweet Potato and Leek Hash, 114
    Zucchini and Leek with Roasted Garlic Soup, 141

M
mango
    Apricot-Mango Salsa, 76
    Coconut Lime Fruit Salad, 125
    Grilled Chicken Salad with Mango and Avocado, 44
Marinara Sauce, 152
Mayonnaise, Paleo, 150
meal plan, 9–11
meatballs
    Greek-Style Lamb Meatballs, 80
Meatloaf, Yummy Homestyle, 63
Mediterranean Cod, 91
muffins
    Bacon and Egg Omelet Muffins, 24
    Paleo Pumpkin Muffins, 169
mushrooms
    Beef and Veggie Kebabs with Spicy Mediterranean Marinade, 66–67
    Cran-Apple Chicken Salad, 97
    Paleo Chicken and Mushrooms, 50
    Portobello Burger, 58

O
omelet
    Bacon and Egg Omelet Muffins, 24
    Paleo Vegetable Omelet, 16

P
Paleo diet
    7-day meal plan, 9–11
    about, 1–2
    health benefits of, 2–3
    stocking kitchen for, 5–7
pancakes
    Coconut Flour Pancakes, 23
    Paleo Pumpkin Pancakes, 26
    Zucchini Pancake Fritters, 118
pantry items, 5–7
Pecan-Crusted Fish with Orange Salsa, 89
peppers
    Beef and Veggie Kebabs with Spicy Mediterranean Marinade, 66–67
    Beef and Veggie Stir Fry wth Ginger-Orange Sauce, 60
    Italian-Style Tuna Stuffed Peppers, 86
    Roasted Balsamic Vegetables, 124
    Roasted Pepper Stuffed with Spinach, Walnuts, and Ground Beef, 64
    Smoked Salmon Stuffed and Bacon Wrapped Sweet Peppers, 110
    Teriyaki Chicken Stir-Fry, 48
    Zucchini, Red Pepper, and Sweet Potato Frittata, 18
    Zucchini and Red Pepper Shakshuka, 33
Pesto, Basil, 149
pork
    Glazed Pork Chops with Apricot-Mango Salsa, 76

Paleo Breakfast Sausage, 79
Paleo Chili, 56
Slow-Cooked Pork Carnitas, 74
Slow-Cooker Pork Chili Verde, 78
Spanish Chorizo Stew with Sweet Potatoes and Kale, 75
Yummy Homestyle Meatloaf, 63
Portobello Burger, 58
pumpkin
- Paleo Pumpkin Muffins, 169
- Paleo Pumpkin Pancakes, 26
- Pumpkin and Bacon Soup, 144
- Turkey Pumpkin Chili, 53

R
red pepper. *see* peppers
refrigerator items, 7
ribs
- Asian-Style Short Ribs, 70
- Slow Cooker Short Ribs, 68

S
salads
- Coconut Lime Fruit Salad, 125
- Cran-Apple Chicken Salad, 38
- Egg Salad, 28
- Grilled Chicken Salad with Mango and Avocado, 44
- Healthy, Yummy Real Tuna Salad, 96

salmon
- Citrus Baked Salmon, 88
- Pan-Seared Salmon on Baby Arugula, 105
- Smoked Salmon Stuffed and Bacon Wrapped Sweet Peppers, 110
- Wasabi Salmon Burgers, 100

salsa
- Apricot-Mango Salsa, 76
- Fresh Tomato Salsa, 148

sauces
- Basil Pesto, 149
- Ginger-Orange Sauce, 60
- Honey Mustard Sauce, 40, 153
- Marinara Sauce, 152

Scallops with Herb Butter Sauce, Seared, 108
seafood, *see also* fish

Grilled Shrimp Spiced with Homemade Sriracha, 102–103
Lemony Garlic Shrimp over Zoodles, 94
Sautéed Goan Clams, 111
Seared Scallops with Herb Butter Sauce, 108
Shrimp and Avocado Ceviche, 92

shrimp
- Asian Shrimp and Coconut Soup, 136
- Grilled Shrimp Spiced with Homemade Sriracha, 102–103
- Lemony Garlic Shrimp over Zoodles, 94
- Shrimp and Avocado Ceviche, 92

Smoothie, Banana Apple with Greens, 30
soups and stews
- Asian Shrimp and Coconut Soup, 136
- Beef Stew with Butternut Squash, 62
- Chicken, Zucchini, and Carrot Soup, 140
- Cream of Broccoli Soup, 138
- Curried Chicken Stew, 41
- Easy Chicken, Kale, and Carrot Soup, 137
- Paleo Avgolemono, 143
- Paleo Chili, 56
- Pumpkin and Bacon Soup, 144
- Spanish Chorizo Stew with Sweet Potatoes and Kale, 75
- Spiced Ginger Carrot Soup, 134
- Turkey Pumpkin Chili, 53
- Zucchini and Leek with Roasted Garlic Soup, 141

Spanish Chorizo Stew with Sweet Potatoes and Kale, 75
spinach
- Banana Apple Smoothie with Greens, 30
- Crab and Spinach-Stuffed Mushrooms, 97
- Easy Paleo Breakfast Scramble, 20
- Roasted Pepper Stuffed with Spinach, Walnuts, and Ground Beef, 64

squash
- Beef and Veggie Kebabs with Spicy Mediterranean Marinade, 66–67
- Beef Stew with Butternut Squash, 62
- Roasted Balsamic Vegetables, 124

Stir-Fried Vegetables with Toasted Cumin Seeds, 117
sweet potatoes
- Ground Turkey and Sweet Potato Casserole, 52
- Spanish Chorizo Stew with Sweet Potatoes and Kale, 75
- Sweet Potato and Coconut Curry, 120
- Sweet Potato and Leek Hash, 114

Zucchini, Red Pepper, and Sweet Potato Frittata, 18

T
Teriyaki Chicken Stir-Fry, 48
Tilapia and Veggies Baked in Parchment, 99
tomatoes
    Baked Eggs with Tomato and Bacon, 22
    Fresh Tomato Salsa, 148
tuna
    Healthy, Yummy Real Tuna Salad, 96
    Italian-Style Tuna Stuffed Peppers, 86
turkey
    Bun-Less Paleo Turkey Burgers, 44
    Ground Turkey and Sweet Potato Casserole, 52
    Turkey Pumpkin Chili, 53

V
vegetables. *see also specific types*
    Roasted Balsamic Vegetables, 124
    Stir-Fried Vegetables with Toasted Cumin Seeds, 117
    Tilapia and Veggies Baked in Parchment, 99

W
Wasabi Salmon Burgers, 100

Z
zucchini
    Chicken, Zucchini, and Carrot Soup, 140
    Curried Zucchini Chips, 157
    Lemony Garlic Shrimp over Zoodles, 94
    Roasted Balsamic Vegetables, 124
    Slow Cooker Beef Ragu with Zoodles, 59
    Zoodles, 115
    Zucchini, Red Pepper, and Sweet Potato Frittata, 18
    Zucchini and Leek with Roasted Garlic Soup, 141
    Zucchini and Red Pepper Shakshuka, 33
    Zucchini Pancake Fritters, 118

www.ingramcontent.com/pod-product-compliance
Lightning Source LLC
Chambersburg PA
CBHW061148070526
44584CB00034B/4457